SSI Monograph

DRUG TRAFFICKING, VIOLENCE, AND INSTABILITY

Phil Williams
Vanda Felbab-Brown

April 2012

FOREWORD

Over the past 2 years, the Strategic Studies Institute (SSI) and the University of Pittsburgh Matthew B. Ridgway Center for International Security Studies (Center for Latin American Studies and Office of the Provost) have conducted two conferences: The first was entitled "Drug Trafficking, Violence, and Instability in Mexico, Colombia, and the Caribbean: Implications for U.S. National Security," and the second was "Violent Armed Groups: A Global Challenge."

Keynote speakers for the first conference were: Bruce Bagley, Professor and Chair, Department of International Studies, University of Miami and Director, University of Miami's Center of Latin American Studies, who addressed "What Can the Mexican State Do to Combat Organized Crime?"; and Jorge Chabat, Professor/Investigator, Centro de Investigación y Docencia Económicas (Center for Research and Teaching in Economics), who discussed "The Drug War in Mexico: Dilemmas and Options." Speakers for the second conference included Dr. Robert Mandel, Professor of International Affairs at Lewis & Clark College, and John Robb, author of the book *Brave New War*. Dr. Mandel addressed "Global Security Upheaval: Armed Non-State Groups as Stability Enhancers," and Mr. Robb addressed "The Bazaar of Violence."

The conference sponsors found the presentations at the two conferences to be sufficiently complementary to combine them in a series of monographs under the main title of Violent Armed Groups. Specific monographs within the series will have subtitles encompassing groups of works selected from among the presentations by the four keynote speakers and over 40 panelists. The introduction to this first monograph,

"Drug Trafficking, Violence, and Instability," will serve to: (1) introduce the series by providing general conceptions of the global security challenges posed by violent armed groups; (2) identify the issues of greatest import to scholars studying the phenomenon; and, (3) emphasize the need for the U.S. Government to understand variations in the challenges it faces from a wide range of potential enemies.

In this first report, Dr. Phil Williams and Dr. Vanda Felbab-Brown provide the strategic context for the series and highlight many of the issues that will be addressed in more detail by authors of subsequent monographs in the series. SSI is pleased to offer this report in fulfillment of its mission to assist U.S. Army and Department of Defense senior leaders and strategic thinkers in understanding the key issues of the day.

DOUGLAS C. LOVELACE, JR.
Director
Strategic Studies Institute

ABOUT THE AUTHORS

PHIL WILLIAMS is the Wesley W. Posvar Professor and Director of the Matthew B. Ridgway Center for International Security Studies at the University of Pittsburgh. His previous assignments included Visiting Professor at the Strategic Studies Institute, U.S. Army War College; and Visiting Scientist at CERT Carnegie Mellon University, where he worked on cyber-crime and infrastructure protection. Dr. Williams has worked extensively on transnational criminal networks, terrorist networks, terrorist finances, and has focused most recently on the rise of drug trafficking violence in Mexico. He has published extensively in the field of international security. He has written many books on the field of international security including: *Crisis Management* (1976); *The Senate and U.S. Troops in Europe* (1986); and, (with Mike Bowker) *Superpower Detente: A Reappraisal* (1987); along with a number of edited volumes on Russian organized crime, trafficking in women, and combating transnational crime. Dr. Williams is also the author of *From the New Middle Ages to a New Dark Age: The Decline of the State and U.S. Strategy* (Strategic Studies Institute, U.S. Army War College, 2008) and *Criminals, Militias and Insurgents: Organized Crime in Iraq* (Strategic Studies Institute, U.S. Army War College, 2009). He also co-authored (with James Cockayne) *The Invisible Tide: Towards an International Strategy to Deal with Drug Trafficking Through West Africa* (International Peace Institute, 2009).

VANDA FELBAB-BROWN is a Fellow in the Latin America Initiative and in the 21st Century Defense Initiative in Foreign Policy at the Brookings Institution. She is an expert on international and internal conflict issues and their management, particularly on the interaction between illicit economies and military conflict. She focuses on South Asia, Burma, the Andean region, Mexico, and Somalia. Dr. Felbab-Brown is the author of *Shooting Up: Counterinsurgency and the War on Drugs* (Brookings Institution Press, December 2009), as well as numerous policy reports, academic articles, and opinion editorials. A frequent commentator in U.S. and international media, Dr. Felbab-Brown also regularly testifies on these issues before the U.S. Congress.

INTRODUCTION

The rationale for this series is a reflection of the ways in which the world of armed groups has changed and is continuing to change, and the impact of these changes on threats and challenges to national and global security. Although challenges posed by various kinds of violent armed groups initially appear highly diverse and unrelated to one another, in fact they all reflect the increasing connections between security and governance — and, in particular, the relationship between poor governance and violent armed groups. The growth in the number of states with capacity gaps, functional holes, and legitimacy deficits helps to explain the resurgence of a new medievalism, and the rise of illegal quasi-governments in localized areas. The irony is that after several decades in which the number of sovereign states represented in the United Nations (UN) has increased significantly, relatively few of these states can truly claim a monopoly on force within their territorial borders.

Violent challengers to the Westphalian state have taken different forms in different parts of the world. These forms include tribal and ethnic groups, warlords, drug trafficking organizations, youth gangs, terrorists, militias, insurgents, and transnational criminal organizations. In many cases, these groups are overtly challenging the state; in others they are cooperating and colluding with state structures while subtly undermining them; in yet others, the state is a passive bystander while violent armed groups are fighting one another. The mix is different, the combinations vary, and the perpetrators of violence have different motives, methods, and targets. In spite of their divergent forms, however, nonstate violent actors share certain qualities and characteristics. As Roy Godson and Richard Shultz have pointed out, "As surprising as it may seem, pirate attacks off Somalia, militias in Lebanon, and criminal armies in Mexico are part of a global pattern and not anomalies." Indeed, these violent armed groups or, as they are sometimes called, violent non-state actors (VNSAs) represent a common challenge to national and international security, a challenge that is far greater than the sum of the individual groups, and that is likely to grow rather than diminish over the next several decades. Although the U.S. military — especially the Air Force and the Navy — still place considerable emphasis on the potential emergence of peer competitors among foreign armed forces, more immediate challenges have emanated not from states but from various kinds of VNSAs.

Most obviously, on September 11, 2001 (9/11), the United States became the target of extremist Islamic terrorist organizations based overseas. It has subsequently had to confront the homegrown offshoots of these groups. Most immigrants to the United States bring with them an allegiance to their new home; a small minority, however, retains allegiance to other entities and causes. Moreover, there are a small but growing number of cases in which American citizens go abroad to fight with extremist groups or to receive training so that they can return and carry out attacks on American soil. Although the killing of Osama bin Laden is seen by some observers as the beginning of the end for al-Qaeda, the threat posed by extremist Islamic terrorist organizations is likely to be far more enduring than any single individual or organization.

U.S. military interventions in both Iraq and Afghanistan have been compelled to confront insurgencies and terrorist groups that have proved to be both more agile and more resilient than anticipated by many analysts. The counterinsurgency efforts in Iraq had some remarkable successes in 2007 and 2008, but with U.S. forces drawing down, questions remain about Iraq's long-term stability. The insurgency in Afghanistan has also proved to be a devilish challenge, making it difficult to replicate there even the partial success in Iraq. In both instances, corruption in government has complicated and undermined the efforts to defeat the insurgency, while the insurgents have used a wide variety of criminal activities to fund their political and military campaigns. In Afghanistan, the Taliban has benefited enormously from its linkages with the opium and heroin industry and has been able to make a comeback using profits generated through taxation of farmers, protection of drug shipments, deployment of mobile laboratories, and a minor role in trafficking.[1] Moreover, the problems of governance in Afghanistan are compounded by involvement of government officials and/or their family members in the drug business and by corruption—factors that are as pervasive as they are debilitating.

Drugs have funded insurgency not only in Afghanistan but also in countries as diverse as Colombia and Burma. Moreover, the drug industry has proved both resilient and adaptive. As the situation in Colombia has improved with the destruction of large drug trafficking organizations with a high degree of vertical integration, it has deteriorated in Mexico. As Mexican drug trafficking organizations have come to dominate wholesale markets in the United States, so the drug trafficking organizations in Mexico have become increasingly powerful and increasingly ruthless in their competition with one another. Indeed, the United States is facing a massive upsurge of drug-related violence on its southern border. Most of this is internecine violence among Mexican drug trafficking organizations themselves; some is directed against the Mexican government. The major Mexican drug trafficking organizations have a presence in almost all major U.S. cities and are closely linked to many gangs.[2] According to a Congressional Research Service Report, however, the spillover of violence from Mexico to the United States predicted by many observers has not yet materialized fully, even though its potential is significant.[3]

The United States has already experienced an influx of criminal organizations from countries as diverse as Russia, Albania, Colombia, Mexico, Nigeria, China, and Vietnam. This is not surprising. The United States (with the European Union close behind) is the most attractive market or host state for criminals seeking lucrative criminal opportunities. These opportunities can stem from factors as different as the demand for illicit drugs, the growth of electronic commerce, and the difficulties faced by law enforcement agencies when dealing with foreign groups able to use language and dialects as defense mechanisms. Consequently, the pattern of ethnic succession in organized crime in the United States has broadened into a diverse and sometimes bewildering kaleidoscope, with many of the emergent organizations maintaining criminal linkages in their state of origin.

The global commons (in both cyber-space and the oceans) has been subject to criminal behavior with serious direct and indirect implications for the United States.[4] Because of the lack of a viably effective government in Somalia, Somali pirates are able to operate with a high degree of impunity, seizing and ransoming ships and crews moving through the Gulf of Aden. U.S. ships—as was evident with the seizure of the cargo ship, *Maersk Alabama*—are as vulnerable to such actions as those of any other state. Legal and regulatory asymmetries, while not as pronounced as state absence, can have a similar impact, enabling cyber-criminals, for example, to operate from safe havens, targeting individuals, financial institutions, and businesses in the United States and other countries.

Although these threats to national security are increasingly recognized, U.S. Government institutions and agencies are still in the process of adapting to them. Moreover, the U.S. military, including the Army, must adapt in a period of significant budgetary constraint. It is all the more important, therefore, that we understand the adversaries that we have to confront. This series is designed primarily to assist this process of knowing the enemies.

This first monograph, "Drug Trafficking, Violence, and Instability," focuses on the complex relationship between human security, crime, illicit economies, and law enforcement. It also seeks to disentangle the linkages between insurgency on the one hand and drug trafficking and organized crime on the other, suggesting that criminal activities help sustain an insurgency, but also carry certain risks for the insurgency.

Subsequent monographs will focus on specific areas where violent armed groups operate, or they will delve into specifics about some of those groups. Some works will be descriptive or historical, while others are more analytical, but together they will clarify the security challenges that, arguably, are the most important now faced by the United States and the rest of the world. The series will include monographs on Mexico, the Caribbean, and various kinds of violent armed groups.

ENDNOTES - INTRODUCTION

1. See *Addiction, Crime and Insurgency: The Transnational Threat of Afghan Opium*, Vienna, Austria: UN Office on Drugs and Crime, October 2009.

2. National Drug Intelligence Center, *National Drug Threat Assessment 2010*, Washington, DC: Department of Justice, Product No. 2010-Q317-001, February 2010.

3. Kristin M. Finklea, William J. Krouse, and Marc R. Rosenblum, *Southwest Border Violence: Issues in Identifying and Measuring Spillover Violence*, Washington, DC: Congressional Research Service, August 25, 2011.

4. Scott Jasper, *Securing Freedom in the Global Commons*, Palo Alto, CA: Stanford University Press, 2010.

CHAPTER 1

FIGHTING THE NEXUS OF ORGANIZED CRIME AND VIOLENT CONFLICT WHILE ENHANCING HUMAN SECURITY

Vanda Felbab-Brown

Human insecurity has greatly intensified over the past 2 decades in many parts of Latin America. To an unprecedented degree, ordinary people in the region complain about living in fear of crime. With the exception of Colombia, criminal activity throughout the region has exploded. Doubling since the 1980s, homicide rates in Latin America are among the highest in the world. Kidnapping is also frequent. Well above 50 percent of the approximately 7,500 worldwide kidnappings in 2007 took place in Latin America.[1] Overall, the rates of violent crime are six times higher in Latin America than in the rest of the world.[2] With over 6,000 deaths reported in 2008 and over 6,500 in 2009, drug-related violence in Mexico each year has surpassed conflict-caused deaths in both Afghanistan and Iraq, two countries in the midst of civil war.[3] In 2011, 12,903 drug-related violence deaths were recorded, and over 50,000 since President Felipe Calderón took office.[4] Organized crime is one of the principal sources of threats to human security, but so is flourishing street crime, which frequently receives far less attention from governments—whether the United States Government or national governments in Latin America and the Caribbean. Indeed, law enforcement in Latin America is clearly struggling to cope with both organized and street crime, while 2 decades of efforts to improve and reform law enforcement institutions have little

1

to show in the way of improvements in public safety and accountability of law enforcement. Many Latin Americans are deeply distrustful of and dissatisfied with their local law enforcement institutions.[5]

Yet, despite the clearly negative effects of high levels of pervasive street and organized crime on human security, the relationship among human security, crime, illicit economies, and law enforcement is highly complex. Human security includes not only physical safety from violence and crime, but also economic safety from critical poverty, social marginalization, and fundamental under-provision of such elemental social and public goods as infrastructure, education, health care, and rule of law. Chronically, Latin American governments have been struggling in their efforts to provide all these public goods in large parts of their countries, both rural and urban. These multifaceted institutional weaknesses are at the core of why the relationship between illegality, crime, and human security is so complex. By sponsoring illicit economies in areas of state weakness where legal economic opportunities and public goods are seriously lacking, crime groups frequently enhance some elements of human security even while compromising others. At the same time, simplistic law enforcement measures can and frequently do further degrade human security. These pernicious dynamics become especially severe in the context of violent conflict.

This analysis will focus particularly on the general dynamics of the drug-violence nexus and the role of belligerent actors and crime groups. It introduces illustrations from Latin America and assesses the intensity of threats to U.S. national security emanating from this nexus in Latin America and elsewhere in the world. The chapter concludes with recommendations for U.S. policies in dealing with the threats to U.S. national security from organized crime while at the same time enhancing human security.

DYNAMICS OF THE DRUG-INSECURITY NEXUS

A variety of actors have penetrated various illicit economies, including the drug trade, usually considered the most lucrative of illicit economies and estimated to generate revenues on the order of hundreds of billions of dollars a year. An illicit economy means any economy that supplies commodities or services the production and marketing of which are either completely prohibited by governments and/or international organizations, or partially proscribed unless the production and marketing comply with special licenses, certification, taxation, and other economic and political regulations.

Actors that participate in illicit economies include the populations that produce the illicit commodities and services; crime groups such as drug trafficking organizations and mafias; belligerent actors such as terrorist, insurgent, and paramilitary groups; and corrupt government and law enforcement officials. The penetration of the illicit economies by terrorist or insurgent groups provides an especially potent threat to states and regional stability since, unlike criminal organizations that usually have more limited aims, such belligerent groups typically seek to eliminate the existing state's presence in particular locales or countries.

Burgeoning and unconstrained drug production and other illicit economies thus have profound negative consequences for states and local stability. Most fundamentally, illicit economies provide an opportunity for belligerent groups to increase their power along multiple dimensions not simply by gaining control of physical resources, but also by obtaining support from local populations.[6] Such belligerents hence pose a serious security threat to local governments and, depending on the objectives of the group, to regional and global security and U.S. interests as well. With large financial profits, the belligerent groups improve their fighting capabilities by increasing their physical resources, hiring greater numbers of better paid combatants, providing them with better weapons, and simplifying their logistical and procurement chains.

Crucially and frequently neglected in policy considerations, such belligerents derive significant political capital—legitimacy with and support from local populations—from their sponsorship of the drug economy. They do so by protecting the local population's reliable (and frequently sole source of) livelihood from the efforts of the government to repress the illicit economy. They also derive political capital by protecting the farmers from brutal and unreliable traffickers, by bargaining with traffickers for better prices on behalf of the farmers, by mobilizing the revenues from the illicit economies to provide otherwise absent social services such as clinics and infrastructure, as well as other public goods, and by being able to claim nationalist credit if a foreign power threatens the local illicit economy. In short, sponsorship of illicit economies allows nonstate armed groups to function as security providers and economic and political regulators. They are thus able to transform themselves from mere violent actors to actors that take on proto-state functions.

Although the political capital such belligerents obtain is frequently thin, it is nonetheless sufficient to motivate the local population to withhold intelligence on the belligerent group from the government if the government attempts to suppress the illicit economy. Since accurate and actionable human intelligence is vital for success in counterterrorist and counterinsurgency efforts as well as law enforcement efforts against crime groups, such withholding seriously undermines the efficacy of government policies.

Four factors determine the amount of political capital which belligerent groups obtain from their sponsorship of illicit economy: the state of the overall economy; the character of the illicit economy; the presence (or absence) of thuggish traffickers; and the government response to the illicit economy.

- The state of the overall economy — poor or rich — determines the availability of alternative sources of income and the number of people in a region who depend on the illicit economy for their basic livelihood.
- The character of the illicit economy — labor-intensive or not — determines the extent to which the illicit economy provides employment for the local population. The cultivation of illicit crops, such as poppy in Afghanistan and coca in Colombia, is very labor-intensive and can provide employment to hundreds of thousands to millions of people in a particular country. Production of methamphetamines such as that sponsored by the United Wa State Army in Myanmar, on the other hand, is not labor-intensive and provides livelihoods for many fewer people.
- The presence (or absence) of thuggish traffickers and the government response to the illicit

economy (which can range from suppression to laissez-faire to rural development) determine the extent to which the population depends on the belligerents to preserve and regulate the illicit economy.

In a nutshell, supporting the illicit economy will generate the most political capital for belligerents when the state of the overall economy is poor, the illicit economy is labor intensive, thuggish traffickers are active in the illicit economy, and the government has adopted a harsh strategy, such as eradication, even in the absence of legal livelihoods and alternative opportunities.

But that does not mean that sponsorship of labor non-intensive illicit economies brings the anti-government belligerents no political capital. If a labor non-intensive illicit economy, such as drug smuggling in Sinaloa, Mexico, generates strong positive spillover effects for the overall economy in that locale by boosting demand for durables, nondurables, and services and hence indirectly providing livelihoods to and improved economic well-being of poor populations, it too can be a source of important political capital. In the Mexican state of Sinaloa, for example, the drug trade is estimated to account for 20 percent of the state's gross domestic product (GDP), and for some of Mexico's southern states, the number might be higher.[7] Consequently, the political capital of the sponsors of the drug trade there, such as the Sinaloa cartel, is hardly negligible.

Moreover, unlike their ideologies, which rarely motivate the wider population to support the belligerents, sponsorship of illicit economies allows belligerent groups to deliver in real time concrete material improvements to lives of marginalized populations. Even when ideology wanes, when the brutality of belligerent groups alienates the wider population and when other sources of support evaporate, this ability to deliver material benefits to the population frequently preserves the belligerents' political capital.

Colombia today provides a clear example. Without doubt, the legitimacy of the leftist guerrilla group, the *Fuerzas Armadas Revolucionarias de Colombia* (Revolutionary Armed Forces of Colombia [FARC]) is, after decades of conflict, at an all-time low. The sources of this decline of political capital are multiple. The political ideology of the group is largely moribund both as a result of global changes and the decline of socialist ideologies as well as the aging and isolation of the FARC's intellectual leadership.[8] The FARC today is under severe pressure from the Colombian military. The brutality of the guerrilla group toward the rural population has progressively increased in the 1990s and 2000s as it competed with rightist paramilitaries. At the same time, the group systematically failed to protect the rural and urban populations against coercion and massacres by the equally and perhaps even more brutal paramilitary groups. Finally, as a result of the demise of the Medellín and Cali cartels in the mid-1990s and the growth in strength of the FARC due to its progressive penetration of the drug trade, the leadership decided to eliminate many traffickers from the territories it controlled and take over their trafficking roles in those territories.[9] By doing so, the group inadvertently eliminated a key source of its political capital. Instead of bargaining on behalf of the *cocaleros* (coca farmers) for better prices for coca paste and mitigating and regulating other forms of the traffickers' abuse against the *cocaleros* as it used to do in the 1980s and early 1990s when independent traffick-ers were present,[10] the FARC put itself in the position of the brutal monopolist that sets prices, limits the customers to whom the population can sell coca paste and base, and inflicts abuse on the rural population.[11]

Yet, to the extent that the state is destroying the il-legal economy on which the local population depends for its basic livelihood, the FARC's political capital still remains sufficient to motivate the population not to provide intelligence on or about the group to the government. Indeed, in areas where coca eradication is intense and legal economic opportunities are lack-ing, human intelligence flows from the broader popu-lation about the FARC are virtually nonexistent, and the *cocaleros* continue to be willing to shield and even join the FARC. Overall, the successes of the Colom-bian military against the FARC have been driven to an unprecedented degree in the context of modern counterinsurgency by signal and image intelligence as supplemented by information from deserters. On the other hand, in areas where coca cultivation and hence eradication are not taking place or where rural liveli-hoods have been prioritized, the human intelligence flows from the population on the FARC are consid-erably higher.[12] Today, as consistently since the early 1980s when the FARC embraced the coca economy, its political capital has been strongest among the *cocale-ros*.

This ability to provide real-time, immediate eco-nomic improvements to the lives of the population on whose support illegal groups depend also ex-plains why even crime groups without ideology can have strong political capital. This will be especially the case if crime groups couple their distribution of material benefits to poor populations with the provision of otherwise absent order and minimal security. By being able to out-compete the state in the provision of governance, organized crime groups can pose significant threats to states in areas or domains where the government's writ is weak and its presence limited.[13] Consequently, the importance of distinctions as to whether a group is a crime group or a political one, or whether belligerents are motivated by profit, ideology, or grievances, is frequently exaggerated in policy discussions.[14]

Policies that focus on degrading the belligerents' physical resources by attempting to destroy the illicit economy are frequently ineffective with respect to the objective of drying up the belligerents' resources. In the case of labor-intensive illicit economies where there are no legal economic alternatives in place, such policies are especially counterproductive with respect to securing intelligence and weaning the population away from the terrorists and insurgents. Eradication of illicit crops has dubious effects on the financial profits of belligerents. Even when carried out effectively, it might not inflict serious, if any, financial losses to the belligerents since effective suppression of the production of the illicit commodity might actually increase the international market price for the commodity. Given continuing demand for the commodity, the final revenues might be even greater. This was, for example, the outcome of the Taliban ban on poppy cultivation in Afghanistan in 2000: after production was suppressed by 90 percent, the value of the Taliban's opium and heroin stocks increased 10 times.[15]

Moreover, the extent of the financial losses of the belligerents also depends on the ability of the belligerents, traffickers, and farmers to store drugs, replant after eradication, increase the number of plants per acre, shift production to areas that are not subject to eradication, or use high-yield, high-resistance crops. Belligerents also have the opportunity to switch to other kinds of illicit activities such as synthetic drugs, illicit logging, gems, illicit trade in wildlife, or fundraising among wealthy sympathetic populations. There has not been one case where eradication bankrupted the belligerent organization to the point of defeating it.

Yet, although the desired impact of eradication — to substantially curtail belligerents' financial resources — is far from certain and is likely to take place only under the most favorable circumstances, eradication will definitely increase the political capital of the belligerents since the local population will all the more strongly support the belligerents and deny the government intelligence.

Policies to interdict drug shipments or anti-money laundering measures are less counterproductive in terms of antagonizing the local populations from the government, but they are extraordinarily difficult to carry out effectively. Most belligerent groups maintain highly diversified revenue portfolios. Attempts to turn off their income are highly intelligence-dependent and resource-intensive. With the exception of some tactical successes in Colombia, such efforts have yet to weaken any significant belligerent group.[16]

Counternarcotics policies therefore have to be weighed very carefully, with a clear eye as to their impact on counterinsurgency and counterterrorism. Seemingly quick fixes such as blanket eradication in the absence of alternative livelihoods, will only strengthen the insurgency and compromise state-building and ultimately counternarcotics efforts themselves.

It is also important to note that some illicit economies and new smuggling methods to which belligerents are pushed as result of suppression efforts against the original illicit economy can have far more dangerous repercussions for global security and U.S. national security than did the original illicit economy. Such alternative sources of financing could involve, for example, obtaining radioactive materials for resale on the black market. Reports that the leftist Colombian guerrilla group, the FARC, acquired uranium for resale so as to offset the temporary fall in its revenues as a result of eradication during early phases of Plan Colombia before coca cultivation there rebounded, is an example of how unintended policy effects in this field can be even more pernicious than the problem they are attempting to address. The FARC's switch to semisubmersibles for transportation of drugs provides another worrisome example of unintended consequences of a policy, this time intensified air and maritime interdiction. The more widespread such transportation technologies are among nonstate belligerent actors, the greater the likelihood that global terrorist groups will attempt to exploit them for attacks against the United States or its assets.

Similarly, in the absence of a reduction of global demand for narcotics, suppression of a narcotics economy in one locale will only displace production to a different locale where threats to U.S. and global security interests may be even greater. Considerations of such second- and third-degree effects need to be built into policy.

Apart from strengthening belligerents and even criminal groups in a multifaceted way, large-scale illicit economies also threaten the security and stability of the state. Politically, they provide an avenue for criminal organizations to enter the political space, corrupting and undermining the legitimate democratic process. These actors, who enjoy the financial resources and political capital generated by sponsoring the illicit economy, frequently experience great success in politics. They are able to secure official positions of power as well as wield influence from behind the scenes. The problem perpetuates itself as successful politicians bankrolled with illicit money make it more difficult for would-be innocent actors to resist participating in the illicit economy, leading to endemic corruption at both the local and national levels. Guatemala, El Salvador, and Haiti are cases in point.[17]

Large illicit economies dominated by powerful traffickers also have pernicious effects on a country's law enforcement and judicial systems. As the illicit economy grows, the investigative capacity of the law enforcement and judicial systems diminishes. Impunity for criminal activity increases, undermining the credibility of law enforcement, the judicial system, and the authority of the government.[18] Powerful traffickers frequently turn to violent means to deter and avoid prosecution, killing or bribing prosecutors, judges, and witnesses. Colombia in the late 1980s and Mexico today are powerful reminders of the corruption and paralysis of law enforcement as a result of extensive criminal networks and the devastating effects of high levels of violent criminality on the judicial system.

In addition, illicit economies have large and complex economic effects.[19] Drug cultivation and processing, for example, generate employment for the poor rural populations and might even facilitate upward mobility. As mentioned above, they can also have powerful macroeconomic spillover effects in terms of boosting overall economic activity. But a burgeoning drug economy also contributes to inflation and can hence harm legitimate, export-oriented, import-sub-

stituting industries. It encourages real estate specu-
lation and undermines currency stability. It also dis-
places legitimate production. Since the drug economy
is more profitable than legal production, requires less
security and infrastructure, and imposes smaller sunk
and transaction costs, the local population is frequently uninterested in, or unable to participate in, other
(legal) kinds of economic activity. The illicit economy
can thus lead to a form of so-called Dutch disease,
where a boom in an isolated sector of the economy
causes, or is accompanied by, stagnation in other core
sectors, since it gives rise to appreciation of land and
labor costs.

EFFECTS OF REGIONAL MANIFESTATIONS OF THE DRUG-CONFLICT NEXUS ON U.S. SECURITY

Even though the drug-conflict nexus follows these
general dynamics irrespective of the locale, how acute
a threat to U.S. security interests it presents depends
on the strategic significance of the state weakened by
such connections and the orientation of the belligerent
group toward the United States.

Perhaps nowhere in the world does the presence
of a large-scaled illicit economy threaten U.S. primary
security interests as much as in Afghanistan. There,
the anti-American Taliban strengthens its insurgency
campaign by deriving both vast financial profits and
great political capital from sponsoring the illicit economy. The strengthened insurgency in turn threatens
the vital U.S. objectives of counterterrorism and Afghanistan's stability plus the lives of U.S. soldiers and
civilians deployed there to promote these objectives.
The large-scale opium poppy economy also under-

mines these goals by fueling widespread corruption of Afghanistan government and law enforcement, especially the police forces.[20]

A failure to prevail against the insurgency will result in the likely collapse of the national government and Taliban domination of Afghanistan's south, possibly coupled with civil war. A failure to stabilize Afghanistan will in turn further destabilize Pakistan, emboldening the jihadists in Pakistan and weakening the resolve of Pakistan's military and intelligence services to take on the jihadists. Pakistan may likely once again calculate that it needs to cultivate its jihadi assets to counter India's influence in Afghanistan — perceived or actual.

But the seriousness of the threat and the strategic importance of the stakes do not imply that aggressive counternarcotics suppression measures taken today will enhance U.S. objectives and global stability. Indeed, just the opposite. Premature measures, such as extensive eradication before legal livelihoods are in place, will simply cement the bonds between the rural population dependent on poppy cultivation for basic livelihood and the Taliban, limit intelligence flows to Afghan and North Atlantic Treaty Organization (NATO) forces, and further discredit the Afghan government and tribal elites sponsoring eradication. Nor, given the Taliban's large sources of other income, will eradication bankrupt the Taliban. In fact, eradication so far has failed to accomplish that while already generating counterproductive outcomes.

After years of an inappropriate focus on eradication of the poppy crop, the new Barack Obama counternarcotics strategy for Afghanistan announced in the summer of 2009, promised to mesh well with the counterinsurgency and state-building effort. By scaling back eradication and emphasizing interdiction and development, it will help separate the population from the Taliban. A well-designed counternarcotics policy is not on its own sufficient for success in Afghanistan, but it is an indispensable condition. Counterinsurgent forces can prevail against belligerents profiting from the drug trade when they increase their own counterinsurgency resources and improve the strategy.

Moreover, "success" in suppressing poppy in Afghanistan might well increase threats to U.S. security in other ways. Given existing global demand, poppy cultivation will shift elsewhere. There are many countries where poppy can be grown; but Burma, which used to be the number one producer for many years, the countries of Central Asia, and Pakistan are likely candidates. A shift to Pakistan would be by far the most worrisome. In that case, Pakistani jihadi groups would not only be able to increase their profits, but also, most dangerously, their political capital. Today, they have little to offer but ideological succor to the unsatisfied populations in the Federally Administered Tribal Areas, the Northwest Frontier Province, and wider Pakistan. If widespread poppy cultivation shifted to these areas, Kashmir, and possibly even parts of Punjab, the jihadist belligerents would be much strengthened by providing real-time economic benefits to marginalized populations.

Drug trafficking organizations in Mexico pose perhaps the second greatest threat to U.S. security on the part of today's actors involved in the global drug trade. Unlike jihadi terrorist groups in Afghanistan and Pakistan, they do not seek to target the U.S. homeland or intend to conduct a deadly terrorism campaign against the United States. Nor do they have the capacity or desire to overthrow the Mexican government. Mexico is not a failing state. But any spillover of the drug war from Mexico could threaten public safety in certain U.S. localities, including substantial increases in murder rates, kidnapping, and other violent crime.

In Mexico, the drug violence has already not only undermined Mexican citizens' human security and overall public safety, but also resulted in suppressed economic activity, including tourism. The provision of public safety is an inescapable and irreducible responsibility of the state, and Mexico is clearly struggling in its delivery. While the political capital of Mexican drug trafficking organizations is limited by their brutality and the fact that the dominant aspect of the drug trade there is labor non-intensive trafficking, they do have political capital that the Mexican government has so far not attempted to counter, focusing instead on narrow interdiction. In Mexico, this political capital comes from the aforementioned spillovers from the illicit economy, the cartels' sponsorship of labor-intensive poppy and cannabis cultivation, and the fact that the cartels now dominate not simply illegal economies but also informal economies in Mexico, such as street sales of CDs in the *Zócalo* (public square) area.[21] Consequently, Mexico's law enforcement strategy needs to be complemented by socio-economic efforts to break the bonds between Mexico's extensive poor and marginalized population and the criminal groups.

Indeed, a focus on the *narcos* and on changing the relationship between the Mexican state and society is now the fourth pillar of the new orientation of the Merida Initiative. The other three pillars of the reoriented strategy include: (1) moving away from high-value targeting of drug trafficking organization *capos* to a more comprehensive interdiction effort that targets the entire drug organization and giving newly trained police forces the primary street security function once again while gradually relegating the military to a background support function; (2) building a secure but smart U.S.-Mexico border that also facilitates trade; and (3) building up Mexico's civilian capacity.[22] The fourth pillar—focused on weaning the population away from the *narcos*—seeks to build resilient communities in Mexico to prevent their takeover by Mexican crime organizations. Through a variety of urban development initiatives, the Mexican government hopes to persuade Mexican citizens who are deeply dissatisfied with the violence that it can better provide them with public goods and social services than can the *narcos*. The effort also aims to restore hope for underprivileged Mexicans—20 percent of Mexicans live below the extreme poverty line, and at least 40 percent of the Mexican economy is informal—that a better future and possibility of social progress lie ahead if they remain in the legal economy. Such bonds between the community and the state are what at the end of the day will allow the state to prevail and crime to attenuate.[23] But these bonds are very hard to build—all the more so given the structural deficiencies of Mexico's economy. To mend these, President Felipe Calderón has unveiled a host of social programs oriented toward bringing jobs, education, and public spaces to Cuidad Juarez. How swiftly and effectively these programs will be implemented remains to be seen.

In Colombia and Africa, the threats to U.S. national security and global stability are comparatively less robust. Colombia is a close U.S. ally, and the United States has accordingly committed over $6 billion to help Colombia achieve security, promote human rights and justice, and reduce the cultivation of illicit crops. While coca in Colombia today remains at levels comparable to or greater than those before intensified aerial spraying began under Plan Colombia, the FARC today is clearly much weakened as a result of the U.S. resources, training, and intelligence provided to the Colombian military.[24] Even though the case of the so-called false positives (civilians shot by the Colombian military and dressed up as guerrillas to show a greater body count) raises serious questions about the military campaign and its successes, security is undeniably better.[25] The demobilization of Colombia's paramilitaries greatly enhanced security and reduced kidnapping in Colombia, even though new paramilitary groups—sometimes referred to as *bandas criminales* (criminal bands) or *grupos emergentes* (emerging paramilitary groups)—are springing up and once again threaten local security. As mentioned before, the FARC's popularity today is lower than ever, but forced eradication without legal alternatives in place unfortunately assures that many *cocaleros* still reject the Colombian state, are willing to put up with the FARC, and are even willing to join the FARC.

Clearly, the United States has an interest in Colombia's enhanced security, prosperity, and human rights promotion. But that country's violent armed groups have not greatly threatened U.S. security interests beyond the FARC's shooting at spraying planes and oil pipelines belonging to U.S. companies. The three U.S. contractors held by the FARC went through a terrible ordeal, and their rescue in 2008 was a joyful moment. But overall, neither the FARC nor the other leftist guerrilla group, the *Ejército de Liberación Nacional* (National Liberation Army [ELN]), have sought to conduct a terrorist campaign against U.S. citizens and major U.S. assets or attack the U.S. homeland. Allegations of al-Qaeda, Hamas, and Hezbollah contacts with the FARC or these groups' penetration of the Latin American drug trade have not proven to be a serious menace.[26]

Similarly, the resurgent *Sendero Luminoso* (Shining Path) in Peru is once again profiting from the drug trade there and once again mobilizing *cocaleros* alienated from the state as a result of eradication. But the group is still comparatively weak and internally oriented.[27]

In Africa, the drug trade clearly threatens the weak states. But once again, while highly worrisome, this threat has not yet affected U.S. security interests or global stability. There is always the possibility that global terrorist groups will seek to exploit African drug trade opportunities for financing and other gains. But terrorist groups can equally seek to exploit legal sources of revenue. Interestingly enough, Somalia's *jihadi al Shabab*, while to some extent tapping into pirates' profits, has not sought to exploit the qat trade between Kenya, Somalia, and the greater Horn of Africa. Instead, *al Shabab* has prohibited both *qat* consumption and trade, thus alienating many Somalis and antagonizing key business interests and power-brokers. So far, however, this has not hampered the group's ability to spread through the country and to threaten the very survival of the government.

OVERALL RECOMMENDATIONS

In conclusion, I can offer several broad policy recommendations:

- Counterinsurgency should not rely on suppression of illicit economies to defeat or even substantially weaken belligerents. Military forces, whether domestic or international, should focus directly on defeating the belligerents and protecting the population. Efforts to limit the belligerents' resources should focus on mechanisms that do not harm the wider population directly, even though such discriminate efforts are difficult to undertake effectively because of their resource intensiveness.

- When dealing with labor-intensive illicit economies in poor countries, governments should undertake suppression efforts that affect the wider population only after military conflict has been brought to an end. Even after the conflict has ended, eradication of illicit crops should be undertaken only when the population has access to effective alternative livelihood programs.
- Efforts to provide legal alternative livelihoods to marginalized poor populations, as painstaking and long-term as they are, should lie at the core of U.S. counternarcotics efforts abroad. Encouraging and extending economic development of the region have to take place not only through steadfast promotion of free trade, but also through determined effort to assist national governments with the development of socioeconomic periphery areas. As the previous 2 decades have shown, free trade on its own does not guarantee that unskilled, poor, marginalized populations in the rural peripheries and urban slums can participate in the global market and reap benefits from it. The United States and Latin American governments should pay greater attention to rural development in the hemisphere as well as to the integration of urban peripheries into the productive and legal

realm of society. If larger segments of the populations are capable of plugging into the global legal economy and see their socioeconomic condition improve, they will depend less on illicit economies and be more willing to cooperate with efforts to reduce them.

- In short, U.S. efforts to suppress violent crime need to be designed to enhance human security in its many facets.
- Interdiction efforts should be designed to limit the coercive and corruptive power of criminal groups rather than to simply and predominantly focus on suppressing the supply of an illicit commodity.
- Governments and international organizations need to consider where the illicit economy is likely to reemerge if suppression efforts in a particular country or region are effective and what the resulting national security and global stability implications will be. Governments and international organizations also need to consider the possibility—including security implications—that if suppression succeeds, other illicit economies will replace the current one.

Governments and their international partners must address the demand for illicit drugs. Such focus on demand reduction in the United States and abroad will not only greatly enhance the U.S. goal of reducing drug consumption, but also best mitigate the dangerous security consequences of the drug-terrorism and drug-insurgency nexus.

ENDNOTES - CHAPTER 1

1. "La industria del secuestro esquilma a América Latina" (The Kidnapping Industry Impoverishes Latin America), *El País*, February 17, 2008.

2. See, for example, Jorge Sapoznikow *et al.*, "Convivencia y Seguridad: Un Reto a la Gobernabilidad" ("Coexistence and Security: A Challenge to Governability"), Washington, DC: Inter-American Development Bank, 2000; and Centro Nacional de Datos, Fondelibertad, Ministrio de Defensa Nacional, República de Colombia, "Cifras Extorcion" ("Extortion Rates"), June 20, 2007; available from *www.antisecuestro.gov.co/documentos/7_16_2007_4_58_07_PM_CifrasHistorias.pdf*.

3. "Ejecutómetro 2010" ("Metrics of Execution 2010"), *Reforma*, accessed April 15, 2010.

4. Cory Molzahn, "Justice in Mexico Monthly News Report," Trans-Border Institute, February 2012, p. 5; Cory Molzahn, Viridiana Ríos, and David A. Shirk, "Drug Violence in Mexico Special Report," Trans-Border Institute, March 2012.

5. See, for example, John Bailey and Lucía Dammert, "Public Security and Police Reform in the Americas," *Public Security and Police Reform in the Americas*, Pittsburgh, PA: University of Pittsburgh Press, 2006, pp. 1-22.

6. This section draws heavily on Vanda Felbab-Brown, *Shooting Up: Counterinsurgency and the War on Drugs*, Washington, DC: Brookings Institution Press, 2009.

7. Guillermo Ibara in Manuel Roig-Franzia, "Mexico's Drug Trafficking Organizations Take Barbarous Turn: Targeting Bystanders," *Washington Post*, July 30, 2008, p. A9.

8. For a discussion of the evolution of the group's ideology, see, for example, Adam Isacson, "Was Failure Avoidable? Learning From Colombia's 1998-2002 Peace Process," *The Dante B. Fascell North-South Center Working Paper Series*, Paper No. 14, March 2003; available from *www.miami.edu/nsc/publications/NSC PublicationsIndex.html#WP*.

9. For trafficking to other parts of the country and the coast, the FARC still relies either on new cartels—the so-called boutique cartels—or on reemergent paramilitary groups, also known as *grúpos emergentes* or *bandas criminales*. While the FARC clearly trades with Mexican drug trafficking organizations, there is little evidence that it has significantly penetrated either international drug trafficking routes or distribution in retail markets.

10. For an excellent discussion of the variety of these regulatory and protective services, see Nazih Richani, *Systems of Violence: The Political Economy of War and Peace in Colombia*, Albany, NY: State University of New York Press, 2002.

11. Felbab-Brown, *Shooting Up*, Chap. 4.

12. Based on author's fieldwork in coca and noncoca areas in Nariño, Magdalena Media, and Montes de Maria, in the Summer and Fall of 2008. See also Vanda Felbab-Brown, Joel M. Jutkowitz, Sergio Rivas, Ricardo Rocha, James T. Smith, Manuel Supervielle, and Cynthia Watson, Management Systems International, *Assessment of the Implementation of the United States Government's Support for Plan Colombia's Illicit Crops Reduction Components*, Washington, DC: U.S. Agency for International Development (USAID), April 2009; available from *pdf.usaid.gov/pdf_docs/PDACN233.pdf*.

13. For seminal work on the governance functions of crime, see Diego Gambetta, *The Sicilian Mafia: The Business of Private Protection*, Cambridge, MA: Harvard University Press, 1993. The literature on organized crime typically assumes that criminal organizations serve one or more of the following functions: economic—the generation of material profit; social—establishment of contacts and promotion of social solidarity; and quasi-governmental—regulating the economic activity not only of their members, but also of other illegal economic competitors within their sphere of influence by establishing and enforcing rules of conduct. See Klaus von Lampe, "Criminally Exploitable Ties: A Network Approach to Organized Crime," Emilio C. Viano, Jose Magallanes, and Laurent Bridel, eds., *Transnational Organized Crime: Myth, Power, and Profit*, Durham, NC: Carolina Academic Press, 2003. See also Phil Williams, "Transnational Criminal Organizations: Strategic Alliances," *The Washington Quarterly*, Vol. 18, No. 1, Winter 1994, pp. 57-72.

14. For a review of these arguments, see, for example, Collier Paul and Anke Hoeffler, "Greed and Grievance in Civil Wars," October 21, 2001; available from *econ.worldbank.org/files/12205_greedgrievance_23oct.pdf*; Román D. Ortiz "Insurgent Strategies in the Post-Cold War: The Case of the Revolutionary Armed Forces of Colombia," *Studies in Conflict and Terrorism,* Vol. 25, 2002, pp. 127-143; Francisco Gutiérrez Sanín, "Criminal Rebels? A Discussion of Civil War and Criminality from the Colombian Experience," *Politics and Society,* Vol. 32, No. 2, June 2004, pp. 257-285; Mats Berdal and David Malone, eds., *Green and Grievance: Economic Agendas in Civil War,* Boulder, CO: Lynne Rienner, 2000; Mats Berdal and David Keen, "Violence and Economic Agendas in Civil Wars: Some Policy Implications," *Millennium: Journal of International Studies,* Vol. 26, No. 3, 1997, pp. 795-818; and Cynthia J. Arnson and I. William Zartman, eds., *Rethinking the Economics of War: The Intersection of Need, Creed, and Greed,* Washington, DC: Woodrow Wilson Center Press, 2005.

15. Vanda Felbab-Brown, "Kicking the Opium Habit? Afghanistan's Drug Economy and Politics Since the 1980s," *Conflict, Security, and Development,* Vol. 6, No. 2, Summer 2006, pp. 127-149.

16. For a detailed discussion of the effects of a range of policies toward illicit economies on the belligerents' physical resources and political capital, see, Felbab-Brown, *Shooting Up,* Chap. 2.

17. See, for example, The Washington Office on Latin America (WOLA), *The Captive State: Organized Crime and Human Rights in Latin America,* WOLA Special Report, October 2007; and James Cockayne and Adam Lupel, eds. "Peace Operations and Organized Crime," Special Issue, *International Peacekeeping,* Vol. 16, No. 1, February 2009.

18. Mónica Serrano and María Celia Toro, "From Drug Trafficking to Transnational Organized Crime in Latin America," Mats Berdal and Monica Serrano, eds., *Transnational Organized Crime and International Security: Business as Usual?* Boulder, CO: Lynne Rienner, 2002, pp. 141-154.

19. See, for example, Francisco E. Thoumi, *Illegal Drugs, Economy, and Society in the Andes*, Baltimore, MD: Johns Hopkins University Press, 2004; Pranab Bardhan, "Corruption and Development: A Review of the Issues," *Journal of Economic Literature*, Vol. 35, No. 3, 1997, pp. 1320-1365; Peter Reuter, "The Mismeasurement of Illegal Drug Markets: The Implications of Its Irrelevance," Susan Pozo, ed., *Exploring the Underground Economy*, Kalamazoo, MI: W. E. Upjohn Institute, 1996, pp. 63-80; and Mauricio Reina, "Drug Trafficking and the National Economy," in Charles Berquist, Ricardo Peñaranda, and Gonzalo Sánchez G., eds., *Violence in Colombia 1990–2000: Waging War and Negotiating Peace*, Wilmington, DE: A Scholarly Resources Inc. Imprint, 2001.

20. Vanda Felbab-Brown, "Peacekeepers Among Poppy," *International Peacekeeping*, Vol. 16, No. 1, February 2009, pp. 100-114.

21. Vanda Felbab-Brown, "The Violent Drug Market in Mexico and Lessons from Colombia," Policy Paper No. 12, Washington, DC: Foreign Policy at Brookings, March 2009, available from *www.brookings.edu/~/media/Files/rc/papers/2009/03_mexico_drug_market_felbabbrown/03_mexico_drug_market_felbabbrown.pdf*.

22. U.S. Ambassador to Mexico, Carlos Pascual, Presentation at Georgetown University, Washington, DC, February 22, 2010.

23. For an evaluation of the new Merida Initiative, *Beyond Merida*, see Vanda Felbab-Brown, "How to Win Mexico's Drug War," *Daily Beast*, March 27, 2010; available from *www.brookings.edu/opinions/2010/0327_mexico_drug_war_felbabbrown.aspx*.

24. Felbab-Brown *et al.*, *Assessment*.

25. Peter DeShazo, Tanya Primiani, and Phillip McLean, "Back from the Brink: Evaluating Progress in Colombia, 1999-2007," Washington, DC: Center for Strategic and International Studies (CSIS), November 2007.

26. See, for example, Rex Hudson, *Terrorist and Organized Crime Groups in the Tri-Border Area (TBA) of South America*, Washington, DC: Report by the Federal Research Division, Library of Congress, July 2003.

27. See, for example, Simon Romero, "Cocaine Trade Helps Rebels Reignite War in Peru," *New York Times*, March 18, 2009.

CHAPTER 2

INSURGENCIES AND ORGANIZED CRIME[1]

Phil Williams

INTRODUCTION

Violence is expensive but can also be highly profitable. Emperors, dictators, and even modern democratic leaders are able to pay for violence by drawing on the resources of those under their territorial and political control. In European history, in particular, warmaking and state-building long went hand in hand.[2] Indeed, the 20th century total wars were as much about the capacity of states to mobilize resources as they were about military strategy — and those with access to the most resources ultimately prevailed.

In contrast, many of the nonstate groups which now challenge states internally or challenge the international status quo, often have very limited access to resources. They are much weaker than states, a difference that has been encapsulated in the notion of asymmetric warfare. Insurgencies, by definition, are engaged in asymmetrical conflict with states. Even though many of these states suffer from capacity gaps, functional holes, and legitimacy deficits — all factors that typically contributed to dissatisfaction and insurgency — they usually have a much larger resource base than insurgents, at least at the outset. In some cases, insurgencies have compensated for their weakness by obtaining access to external resources typically provided by external powers hostile either to the existing government or to the political system within the state and seeking to bring about change without direct confrontation with other great powers. During the Cold War in particular, such arrangements suited the two superpowers and weak regimes, resulting in the prevalence of what might be termed "insurgency by proxy." The results were that insurgencies were rarely short of resources, while the issue of insurgency funding became part of the Soviet-American propaganda battle rather than something to be examined rigorously in its own right.

With the recent insurgencies in Iraq and Afghanistan as well as the continuing insurgency in Colombia, more attention is being given to the funding of insurgencies, to their use of criminal activities, and to their relationships with criminal organizations (especially, but not exclusively, drug trafficking organizations). One of the early pioneers in this area was Steven Metz who, in an important and prescient analysis in 1993, differentiated between spiritual and commercial insurgencies, noting how the Revolutionary Armed Forces of Colombia (FARC) in Colombia was becoming torn between the competing impulses of ideological purity on the one side and the desire to exploit the drug business to expand its revenue base on the other.[3] More recently, Gretchen Peters dissected the linkages between drugs, insurgency, and terror in Afghanistan; Svante Cornell explored the link between drugs and conflict more broadly;[4] and Vanda Felbab-Brown provided a set of detailed and valuable case studies on the links between armed conflict and the drug trade as well as the relationships between counterinsurgency and counternarcotics efforts.[5] Other analysts such as Peter Chalk have explored the criminal activities of the Liberation Tigers of Tamil Eelam (LTTE), while William Noel Ivey titled a chapter on the Naxalite insurgency in India, "Robin Hood or Al Capone?"[6] Another useful set of writings has focused on need, creed, and greed arguments, while the issue of resource extraction or lootable resources has been illuminated by Richard Snyder, who links it explicitly to the outbreak of conflict on the one side and the maintenance of stability on the other.[7] Indeed, Snyder develops a compelling and highly relevant "political economy of extraction framework that explains political order and state collapse as alternative outcomes in the face of lootable wealth."[8]

Progress has also been made in understanding the linkage between terrorism and organized crime, especially since September 11, 2001 (9/11). The focus on terrorist funding has even provided some insights into insurgency funding (although often at the expense of the distinction between terrorist organizations and insurgencies). Tamara Makarenko identified a continuum between terrorism and organized crime, highlighting points of convergence between the two, in ways that were, in some respects, illuminating although not wholly persuasive.

Others who have contributed to the analysis of the connections between terrorism and organized crime include Christopher Dishman, John Picarelli, and Christopher Oehme, while Lyubov Mincheva and Ted Robert Gurr have astutely analyzed points of convergence and divergence between criminal and political organizations and delineated the ways in which the organizations are likely to cooperate.[9] One of the most useful explorations of insurgency and organized crime, however, remains that by R. Thomas Naylor whose dissection of what he terms "the insurgent economy" is full of important insights. Naylor's analysis is somewhat dated but is both incisive and, for the most part, highly compelling.[10] It is complemented by Felbab-Brown's cogent examination of the intersections of insurgencies and the drug business.[11]

It is perhaps all the more surprising, therefore, that even today in many discussions of insurgencies, the themes of funding through criminal activities and links between insurgencies and criminal enterprises are dealt with in a perfunctory manner at best. David Kilcullen in *The Accidental Guerilla*, for example, gives neither issue more than a cursory glance, and there is a danger that one of the major lessons being taken from Iraq is that strategy is critical and resources are secondary.[12] While other analysts of insurgencies are more sensitive to the resource and funding issues, even now there is no general treatment of the relationship between insurgency and organized crime — apart from the works by Naylor and Felbab-Brown — which offers the same kind of illuminating insights as the RAND studies of how insurgencies end or Weinstein's analysis of the organization of insurgent violence.[13]

All this is understandable. There are several conceptual and methodological problems that immediately confront efforts to deal with insurgencies and organized crime. The first is the issue of labeling and distinguishing between insurgency and terrorism. Makarenko solves this by conflating the two.[14] Naylor, in contrast, has argued that terror is only a tactic and that therefore the primary focus should be on insurgencies and guerrilla groups. Since the events of 9/11, however, conflation has become the dominant motif both in academic writings and at the policy level. The distinction between insurgency and terrorism was also blurred by the Bush administration's very broad use of the term terrorist. This tendency was mirrored by some recipients of U.S. aid who confronted insurgencies but saw the utility of labeling them "terrorist threats," echoing the way the communist threat was exploited during the Cold War. Having said this, there can certainly be an overlap between insurgency and terrorism. U.S. forces in Iraq, for example, had to confront what was, in essence, a composite insurgency—or what Thomas Hammes termed a coalition insurgency—in which foreign jihadis affiliated with or inspired by al-Qaeda fought alongside Ba'athist groups and Sunni tribes.[15] At times Shia militia, especially Jaish-al-Mahdi (JAM), also became part of the insurgency. Nevertheless, it remains possible to differentiate between insurgents who see the state as the prize, want to replace the existing government, and are concerned with legitimacy and governance on one hand, and terrorists who tend to pursue less specific and more amorphous objectives on the other. Even with such a differentiation between terrorist and insurgent, considerable fuzziness at the edges is inescapable, especially with nationalist organizations such as the Provisional Irish Republican Army (PIRA) or the Kurdistan Workers' Party (PKK).

These problems are compounded when organized crime is brought into the equation. As suggested above, Makarenko deals with the issue through the articulation of a crime-terror continuum along which criminals and terrorists both use each other's methods and cooperate with one another. This remains one of the most serious efforts to provide a framework of analysis and has been widely adopted. The difficulty with Makarenko's analysis is that the continuum covers both activities and connections—even though these are very different—which are lumped together under the rubric of the crime-terrorism nexus. In contrast, the present author has made a distinction between entities and activities and suggested that "do-it-yourself" organized crime by terrorists is far more important than the linkages between the two kinds of groups.[16] Furthermore, it is when engaging in criminal activities for profit that terrorist groups and networks are most likely to develop cooperative linkages with criminal enterprises. Yet even this is not preordained. The PKK, for example, became deeply involved in drug trafficking in Europe, but rather than cooperating with the traditional Kurdish criminal networks already there, it sought to drive them out of the market and replace them. The relationship between the PKK and Kurdish criminal organizations was characterized not by cooperation but by a series of turf wars over heroin markets in Europe, struggles that the PKK mostly won.[17]

Some observers have responded to questions about the relationship between organized crime and terrorism by resurrecting the term narco-terrorism. The original incarnation of this term referred to drug trafficking organizations—especially those in Medellin—using terror as an integral part of the trafficking enterprise. Yet today narco-terrorism is used primarily to describe insurgent or terrorist organizations using drug trafficking to fund their political campaigns of violence. A term that can be used to describe two very different phenomena is so elastic that it ceases to be helpful—although it is worth noting that in Peru the term narco-terrorism has become enshrined in Article 296-B of the Penal Code.[18] What makes this somewhat ironic is that the term was not entirely appropriate even in the 1990s when Sendero Luminoso (Shining Path) appeared to be working together with drug trafficking organizations in the Upper Huallaga Valley. Although this is often presented as the classic example of alliance between drug traffickers and insurgents, Pablo Dreyfus cautioned very persuasively that it was:

difficult to define the relationship between drug traffickers and Sendero Luminoso as an alliance or even
a "marriage of convenience." The traffickers accepted
Sendero's protection because they did not have a
choice. The insurgents defeated them militarily. Moreover, the pattern of interaction between traffickers and
Sendero was less than beneficial for the traffickers because the insurgents obliged them to pay higher coca
prices to the peasants.[19]

This dynamic seems to have changed, however,
and the comeback of what appears to be a less vicious
Sendero Luminoso is linked to its position as an in-
termediary between Peruvian peasants and Mexican
drug trafficking organizations. Sendero Luminoso has
reemerged in the VRAE, the valley surrounding the
Apurimac and Ene Rivers, which is also the second
largest coca-producing area in Peru. According to
"Comrade Dalton," a high-ranking (now imprisoned)
member of Sendero Luminoso and brother-in-law of
"Comrade Jose," the reputed head of Sendero, the
group maintains a "strategic alliance" with drug traffickers, regarding this as essential for the armed struggle against the government.[20] Some critics, however,
contend that the new "kinder, gentler" Sendero Luminoso is more concerned about profit than politics.

Some commentators, rather than reworking old
terms and giving them a new twist, have coined new
terms. For example, John Sullivan, a very astute commentator on crime, terrorism, and insurgency, has used
the term criminal insurgency to describe the drug-related violence in Mexico.[21] Although this has some appeal, it is misleading. Most drug trafficking violence
stems from a competition among the major trafficking
organizations for control of strategic warehouses in

the major cities along Mexico's northern border and access to the highways into the United States. The development of local consumer markets in Mexico has added another dimension to the competition; so too has the emergence of a younger generation of traffickers. The killings of policemen and soldiers, although certainly not insignificant, represent approximately 10 percent of the total violence. Moreover, most of this violence is targeted in precise rather than indiscriminate ways, with very specific military and law enforcement targets. The major exception—the throwing of grenades into a crowd in Morelia in September 2008—was widely condemned by many trafficking organizations. Nor is there any evidence that the drug trafficking organizations are seeking political power. In effect, what they want is to maintain the space and freedom to carry out their trafficking operations. The aim is to neutralize, intimidate, or render complaisant the Mexican state, not to overthrow it.

None of this, however, makes the violence less horrendous. Indeed, what appears to be a growing carelessness in drug-related violence in Mexico is particularly disturbing. There are indications that violence is becoming an end in itself, or even a form of empowerment for the perpetrators, reminiscent of elemental terrorism without political aims. In effect, the traditional norms of selectivity and restraint in the criminal use of violence are eroding and aberrant forms of behavior are becoming fashionable. In some respects, the increase in what can best be described as anomic violence is more disturbing than a criminal insurgency pursuing political objectives and using purposeful violence to achieve these objectives.

Nevertheless, the search for a new term to encapsulate what is going on in Mexico reflects an important impulse: sometimes changes in the security environment require new assessments and new conceptualizations of security challenges. The difficulty with both old and new labels, however, is that they all too easily become a substitute for unpackaging the relationships between insurgencies and organized crime. Karl Weick and Kathleen Sutcliffe, in particular, emphasize that the essence of mindfulness is to be willing to recognize when old conceptualizations and categorizations are inadequate to capture new realities.[22] The implication is that these relationships need to be examined very thoroughly both to enhance understanding and to identify more effective policy choices. In fact, explorations of the relationships between insurgencies and organized crime go to the heart not only of obvious issues such as insurgency effectiveness and sustainability, but also to questions of identity, legitimacy, organizational structure and cohesion, and organizational transformation.

In this connection, a vexing but important conceptual issue concerns the extent to which insurgencies can be regarded as monolithic—either vertically or horizontally. The natural tendency is to treat an insurgency as a cohesive social movement, when in fact there are often important differences within it from top to bottom, that is, vertically. Followers sometimes diverge from the principles and injunctions of their leaders as command and control prove far more tenuous than in traditional military organizations. Or different components of an insurgency will sometimes differ in their objectives and priorities, that is, horizontally. Where you stand can depend as much on where you fight as on where you sit. As suggested above, the insurgency in Iraq was a composite made up of different elements, some of which were nationalistic and concerned only with eviction of U.S. forces, while others wanted to reestablish Sunni and/or Ba'athist dominance in the country. Even where there is less diversity, divisions might still exist. For example, it is not clear that insurgents who engage in criminal activities are always acting on behalf of the insurgency as a whole. In some instances, criminal fund-raising might be a side activity for personal enrichment. In other cases, all the funds will go to the movement. A third possibility is that the money will be divided, with some kept by the fund-raisers and some donated to the cause. Clearly, resource distribution can have important implications for group cohesion, sometimes strengthening and sometimes weakening it.

Another analytical difficulty concerns the extent to which the appropriate focus should be on the objectives of groups as opposed to the means they use. This is sometimes described as the motives versus methods issue.[23] Even if money is simply a means to an end for insurgencies and an end in itself for criminal organizations, the process of fundraising is much the same. In this sense, the activities of criminal enterprises on the one side and insurgents on the other will often appear very similar. Although these difficulties are unavoidable, they can be overcome by efforts at analytic clarity. Consequently, it is critical to outline the key assumptions underlying the analysis.

The first assumption is that insurgencies are expensive, and that resources therefore matter a great deal. This is true even in the straightforward use of terror, where the costs of planning and implementing an attack often turn out to be much higher than police or observer estimates in the immediate aftermath lead us to believe. Perhaps the best example is the Madrid bombings, where the real cost was somewhere between 43,000 and 54,000 Euros and not the

U.S.$10,000 initially estimated by the United Nations (UN) and repeated endlessly thereafter, even by prominent scholars. The costs of insurgencies are considerable, not least because the insurgents have to act as what Naylor termed "nascent governments" if they are to acquire the level of legitimacy and public support that would make them a serious contender for power.[24] Indeed, most insurgents and some terrorist organizations engage in social provision as a means of legitimizing their violence and mobilizing support.[25] Even if such efforts are relatively modest, the level of resources available to insurgents will have a significant impact on their ability to sustain their campaigns. In this connection, both methods — the use of criminal methods by insurgents and cooperation between insurgents and criminal organizations, especially drug trafficking groups — can be crucial means of resource generation or weapons acquisition.

The second assumption is that organized crime can be understood in two distinct ways — as entities and activities. The entities are criminal enterprises concerned about profit. These groups or organizations are Clausewitzian in the sense that their criminal activities are simply a continuation of business by other means. Organized crime can also be understood as a set of activities. These activities or methods can be appropriated by other nonstate actors and by states. This means that insurgencies can use organized crime activities as a funding mechanism and/or can develop relationships of mutual advantage with criminal enterprises.

As to the third assumption, both insurgencies and criminal organizations are dynamic social actors constantly adapting to new constraints and opportunities and seeking to outwit their adversaries in law enforcement, the military, and intelligence agencies. In effect, they are engaged in a process of competitive adaptation with their adversaries.[26] In addition, such groups often have life cycles, and, to some extent, their activities and their relationships will be determined in part by where in these cycles they are located. In the early stages of an insurgency, for example, "a guerilla group may cooperate with domestic and local criminal organizations on the basis of their shared status as social outcasts and their shared immediate objective."[27] As both groups mature, however, cooperation might be more elusive. One of the reasons for this, as Naylor has argued, is that "mature criminality is compatible with the continued existence of the formal state" whereas "mature insurgency threatens its overthrow."[28] Yet even in these circumstances, it might still be possible for the two groups to engage in some degree of cooperation where there are obvious opportunities for mutual gain.[29] Divergence between what Mincheva and Gurr usefully describe as interest-driven criminal organizations and identity-driven political groups is also a plausible outcome.[30] Under some conditions the challenges for an insurgency of maintaining identity and establishing legitimacy might well supersede the desire for connectivity and cooperation.

Against this background the analysis here seeks to do several things:

- To identify the ways in which insurgencies appropriate the methods of criminal enterprises to fund themselves. Indeed, the next part of this chapter examines the extent to which, and the ways in which, different insurgencies have used criminal activities as a funding mechanism. Although much of this is well known, patterns of commonality and important variations from one insurgency to another need to be identified.

- To explore the spectrum of relationships between insurgents and criminal enterprises. Relationships can be based on some elements of common identity, short-term expediency, or long-term mutual advantage. They can range from what are little more than market transactions or service requirements to enduring strategic alliances.
- To identify and explore the consequences of the appropriation of criminal methods by insurgencies. The chapter suggests that insurgent use of criminal activities for fund-raising is likely to have paradoxical consequences, strengthening insurgency in the short term but compromising or weakening it in the long term. Criminal fund-raising can help insurgencies meet their obligations but is not without risk. The nature of this risk is spelled out in terms of the slippery slope of criminality.

INSURGENCIES APPROPRIATING ORGANIZED CRIME AS A FUNDING MECHANISM

Although it is easy to find historical examples in which insurgents used criminal activities as a funding mechanism, there is no clear baseline. In the Algerian insurgency, for example, a ban on criminal activities such as prostitution and drug trafficking was established, even though several of the leaders of the National Liberation Front (FLN), most especially Ben Bella, had a criminal background.[31] In some ways, however, fighting against colonial powers, often with the support of significant parts of the population, was relatively manageable as the insurgents could obtain shelter and support from the population. They could also expect some financial help from sympathetic external powers. In the case of the FLN, assistance came from Algeria's neighbors. With the end of the Cold War and the loss of superpower funding for proxy-insurgencies, those challenging the state have had to become more self-reliant. Perhaps nothing has contributed more to what Hammes has described as the self-sufficiency of contemporary insurgencies than the growing exploitation of criminal activities.[32]

One of the first techniques in the criminal repertoire adopted by insurgencies is kidnapping.[33] Groups in Mindanao and elsewhere in the Philippines, the Islamic Movement of Uzbekistan, the Taliban, and the *Ejército de Liberación Nacional* (National Liberation Army [ELN]), and FARC in Colombia, have all used kidnapping for ransom as a means of funding. Not only does kidnapping require little investment, it can have high payoffs, especially if it involves the abduction of foreigners.[34] Indeed, in many respects kidnapping is an ideal crime for insurgencies. Kidnapping can generate a climate of fear and intimidation, highlight the inability of the government to maintain security, and provide a major revenue stream. For contemporary insurgencies, kidnapping can even be a powerful strategic weapon. In Iraq, for example, the kidnapping of a Filipino truck driver in July 2004 led the Arroyo government to withdraw its 51-person military contingent a month ahead of time, contributing to a major hiccup in the relationship between Washington and Manila. Yet this was only part of the story. The kidnappers reportedly received a ransom that could have been as high as U.S.$6 million.[35] According to one Iraqi newspaper, the government of the Philippines believed the kidnapping was a purely a political one, only to discover at the end that it was also — and perhaps even primarily—about money.[36] In Iraq, the kidnapping of foreigners proved extremely lucrative as the French, German, and Italian governments paid somewhere in the region of $45 million for the release of hostages.[37] How much of this went to insurgents and how much to jihadi groups is difficult to determine. Somewhat ironically, given the relative lack of attention, the kidnapping of Iraq's own citizens was even more lucrative, particularly at its peak in 2006 when as many as 40 Iraqis a day were abducted, and the profits reached at least $140 million.[38] Once again, there is little, if any, open source information on the distribution of the profits among insurgent and jihadi groups on the one side and kidnapping gangs concerned only about the money on the other. The emergence of kidnapping as a funding mechanism for insurgents is not unique to Iraq. It was also used extensively by Chechen rebels during the 1990s, and has long been a staple activity of FARC in Colombia. More recently, kidnapping for ransom in both Afghanistan and Pakistan has provided an important revenue stream for the Taliban and associated groups.

Although Naylor argues that bank robberies are the other staple activity of insurgencies, particularly in their early stages, other opportunities open up as the insurgents establish a degree of territorial control. The Karen National Liberation Army in Burma, for example, was able to tax clandestine teak exports from the area where the insurgents were established.[39] The FARC in Colombia has become involved in illegal gold mining, with some evidence suggesting that the organization "controlled up to 15 gold mines just in Bolívar department, in northern Colombia. Officials say that in some areas the FARC mines gold directly, whereas in others it extorts 'tax' payments from small-scale, and mainly illegal, miners."[40] In other instances where insurgents obtained a degree of control in border regions, they were able to levy taxes on the smuggling of a variety of commodities: the Kosovo Liberation Army, for example, did this very successfully, collecting cash and sometimes weapons from smuggling organizations.[41] When they engage in extortion of this kind, insurgencies have the characteristics of mafias in the strict sense of the term, as defined by Diego Gambetta, in that they engage in the business of private protection.[42] Similarly:

> in parts of Afghanistan where there is little or no poppy grown, insurgents seem to rely more heavily on kidnapping, shakedowns, and protecting other smuggled goods, ranging from timber and gemstones to people and legal goods like tires and cooking oil.[43]

Sometimes protection can evolve into more direct involvement in exploitation of natural resources and even into participation in smuggling networks. In Colombia, for example, the FARC went into the business of protecting and taxing drug growers in much the same way that it taxed cattle ranchers. Soon, though, FARC's relationship with the drug trade was to become much more intimate. This was a very natural development. As Naylor points out, "the drug trade, in the best of liberal capitalist tradition, attracted guerilla groups regardless of their race, color, creed, or political affiliation."[44] Indeed, FARC's role gradually expanded from protecting and extorting the drug business to becoming directly involved in trafficking. Yet this became a source of some internal contention, with at least three divergent positions emerging: those who were extensively involved in both trafficking and taxing of the drug industry and were led by the 16th

Front, which became the organization's main money-maker; those who were reluctant to traffic in drugs but were willing to extort the drug growers and traffickers through the imposition of "taxes"; and those who wanted nothing to do with the business. The antipathy of this third group to involvement in the drug business seems to have stemmed from concerns that crass commercialism might replace ideological purity in the organization.[45] In the event, though, this group was to lose the battle for the soul of FARC. In April 2000, the Paris-based *Observatoire Geopolitique Des Drogues* (Geopolitical Drug Watch [OGD]) reported that the FARC was taking over the role of the trafficker middlemen, buying coca paste and cocaine base from growers to supply processing labs.[46] This was the "point of no return on the road to criminalizing" the organization.[47] FARC subsequently established itself as a supplier to the Costa criminal organization in Brazil and the Arellano Felix Organization based in Tijuana.

Other fronts also became involved in the drug business, and some members of FARC succumbed to the inevitable temptation of moving downstream in the drug trafficking chain, importing cocaine directly into the United States. In March 2006, for example, the Drug Enforcement Administration (DEA) indicted 50 FARC leaders for drug trafficking and claimed that FARC was supplying more than 50 percent of the world's cocaine and more than 60 percent of the cocaine that enters the United States. [48] In September 2006, two FARC members or associates, Cesar Augusto Perez-Parra and Farouk Shaikh-Reyes, were convicted of drug conspiracy. Reportedly, they were planning to supply 1,000 to 2,000 kilos to Miami every 30 to 45 days.[49] Tovar-Parra, a high-ranking member of the 14th Front of FARC, which had become a key participant in the drug business, was also indicted.[50] Significantly, there has also been some FARC presence in West Africa where countries such as Guinea-Bissau have become key transshipment countries for cocaine being sent to the lucrative European market.[51]

Another insurgent movement that became heavily involved in drug trafficking—this time from Afghanistan through Central Asia—was the Islamic Movement of Uzbekistan (IMU). Some commentators even suggested that the group was more interested in profit than politics and ultimately was little more than a criminal organization using terrorist activities and its annual military campaigns as devices to obscure or protect its drug business.[52] The assessment by the Kyrgyz government that the IMU was responsible for 70 percent of the drugs moving through Central Asia was widely cited, even though the evidence for this assessment was unclear.

Svante Cornell presents a more subtle and persuasive analysis of the divide in the IMU between the military, operational, and transportation wing of the insurgency run by Juma Namangami, and the ideological or spiritual wing led by Tohir Yoldash, a picture of internal divisions not entirely dissimilar from those that bedeviled the FARC.[53] Moreover, many IMU members fought in Afghanistan alongside the Taliban and al-Qaeda. Their ranks were decimated, and Namangami was killed. This suggests that the IMU had at least some commitment to identity politics and could not be dismissed simply as a profit-oriented criminal enterprise. The profit-making activities engaged in by the IMU—which included kidnapping as well as drug trafficking—seem to have been motivated, at least in part, by the desire to fund the political-religious struggle rather than by an unadulterated desire for profit.

Certainly Central Asian governments had a vested interest in characterizing the movement as criminal rather than recognizing it as one of the few channels in the region for expressing legitimate dissent.

The linkage between insurgency and the drug business is also relevant in Afghanistan. The opium economy in Afghanistan, though, was well established by the 1990s, and in 1993 Uzbek Customs seized 1.3 metric tons of pure heroin at a border crossing from Afghanistan.[54] Although the extent of Taliban involvement in the drug business was partially obscured by the opium ban in 2000, it seems clear that, like the FARC, it imposed taxes on those involved. In fact, when the Taliban was in power, the tax on opium was one of its few enduring sources of income. As the Taliban has sought to regain power, its involvement in the drug business has expanded. This growing involvement was probably facilitated by the structure of the resurgent Taliban as "a loose alliance in which each region was responsible for raising its own funds."[55]

If this is so, it accords at least partially with Naylor's argument that "the danger of criminalization of motive is particularly acute when individual militants are allowed to run their own enterprises or rackets in exchange for kicking back a certain sum to the group as a whole."[56] By 2004, Taliban teams were attacking checkpoints or making diversionary strikes to protect opium cultivation; by 2007, major commanders were reportedly running their own mobile laboratories to process heroin.[57] Press reports have also suggested that some members of the Taliban have gone a step further and traded heroin for weapons with Russian criminal organizations.

This clearly reflects a dynamic similar to that exhibited by FARC. Indeed, it is possible to identify what can be described as a stairway process whereby insurgents become progressively more involved in the drug business — although it should be acknowledged that prior steps are not prerequisites. Some insurgent groups and/or their supporters are likely to get involved in the trafficking stage even if they are not co-located with the cultivation and processing of narcotics. A good example is LTTE involvement in drug trafficking. Starting in the early 1980s, Tamils began trafficking in drugs in order to finance the political struggle in Sri Lanka. Tamil traffickers were responsible for significant caches of heroin seized in Switzerland, leading Swiss authorities to focus on what they dubbed the "Tamil connection."[58] The peak years for arrests of Tamil drug traffickers were 1984 (317) and 1985 (374). In 1986 the number of arrests went down to 218, and by 1990 it was only 37.[59]

Although there does not seem to have been a resurgence of Tamil drug trafficking in Europe since then, the drug market in Sri Lanka itself continued to expand, with some estimates suggesting that there were over 100,000 users by the end of the 1990s. If we accept that there is considerable flexibility rather than a single uniform pattern for insurgencies co-located with drug cultivation, the key steps are typically as follows:

- The assertion of territorial control over regions in which botanical drugs are cultivated.
- The protection of those who are involved in cultivation against government interference with their activities. In some cases, those involved in cultivation or processing move into insurgent-controlled territory in order to obtain protection against the state rather than the insurgents expanding to incorporate the growers and processors.

- The imposition of fees or taxes for these protection activities.
- Payments by traffickers who come to the region to pick up the product in return for protection against government interference.
- Protection of processing activities.
- Direct involvement in processing.
- Supply to traffickers in other countries (sometimes for money, sometimes barter for guns).
- Direct involvement in the trafficking business.

In this final step, the insurgents develop a fully integrated criminal enterprise that extends into the wholesale market in host states. Several observations are worth emphasizing here. First, this final step might not be an easy one to take. With FARC, it probably resulted from the coincidence of increasing involvement in the drug business, with the destruction of the major vertically integrated organizations in Medellin and Cali that for so long dominated cocaine trafficking to the United States and the subsequent flattening of the Colombian supplier base. Second, this final step is attractive and alluring. As Naylor observed, "To collect truly impressive sums, a guerilla group would have to become directly involved at least with the export traffic in finished product, and it would be best if it could participate in the actual marketing of the refined material inside countries of final destination."[60] Whether the Taliban has either the inclination or the capacity to do something similar is not clear.

Yet, there is an additional factor here. Just as the name of the game in Colombia was cocaine, in Afghanistan, it is opium and heroin. And it is not only insurgents who are involved. When the state, for whatever reason, is weak and there is a dominant commodity — or what some writers have termed a lootable resource — much of the crime, violence, and corruption in the state centers on that commodity. This seems to hold true whether it is opium and heroin in Afghanistan, cocaine in Colombia, diamonds in Sierra Leone, or oil in Iraq.

Moreover, at least three different kinds of players are often linked in a complex matrix of intersecting and overlapping networks: criminals interested in profit; insurgents seeking funding for their political/ideological cause; and corrupt officials and other players within the government who use their position to obtain rents.[61] Sometimes these three distinct groups compete with one another, at other times they either develop specific forms of cooperation or engage in tacit agreement not to interfere with each other's activities. In Afghanistan, for example, members of the Karzai government, including the President's half-brother, have been deeply implicated in one way or another with the drug trade. Indeed, any notion that only the Taliban is involved in the opium business and that a monolithic unified government is trying to suppress this business is a distortion of reality. In Afghanistan, opium is common currency, a source of power and influence, a driver of symbiotic relationships, and a place where corrupt government officials, tribal networks, Taliban insurgents, and transnational drug trafficking organizations overlap and intersect. Corrupt officials at all levels help to facilitate the business.

A similarly pervasive culture of corruption developed in Iraq after the 2003 invasion. For the Iraqi insurgency and for corrupt officials, the equivalent of the opium resource in Afghanistan was oil and petroleum products. The theft, diversion, smuggling, and black market sales of oils became a source of funding for a variety of groups involved in violent conflict. There were at least three different dimensions to this.[62]

1. The theft and diversion of crude oil and its smuggling from the Al Basra Oil Terminal or through the Shat-al-Arab Waterway to the United Arab Emirates (UAE) and as far away as India. Some of this smuggling was done through a process of oil bunkering similar to that in the Niger Delta in which small vessels transferred their loads to oil tankers at sea. Both tribes and corrupt officials were involved. This tended to be a Shia-dominated activity, simply because there were relatively few Sunnis in Basra. There was also considerable competition among the Shia parties and militias for the "rents" which could be obtained, and this often spilled over into violence. Jaish-al-Mahdi, which at times tacitly allied with Sunni insurgents in attacks on Coalition forces yet also engaged in sectarian cleansing of Sunnis (especially in Baghdad), became a key player in providing protection for oil smuggling as did the Fadhila Party.[63]

2. Sunni insurgents also became involved in looting the oil resource, diverting refined products from the country's most important refinery at Bayji and hijacking oil trucks at multiple points along Iraq's insecure highways. They were helped by officials at the refinery and by officials in the Ministry of Oil.[64]

3. Diversion of oil and petroleum products in transit is the third dimension of oil looting. This was facilitated by a system in which there was no coordinated supervision—let alone centralized control—over legitimate transactions and shipments of oil and petroleum from one part of Iraq to another. The attractiveness of diversions was even greater because Iraq had to import refined products to meet demand. These

imported fuels were then sold to Iraqi gas stations at prices subsidized by the government. The fuels could also be stolen and sold on the black market or could be re-exported to Iraq's neighbors where prices were higher.[65]

In sum, where resources can be stolen, diverted, and smuggled, insurgents can take control of the commodity and develop major illicit revenue streams. Indeed, when the product is something like diamonds or oil, the steps are fewer than in the illicit drug industry, and insurgent control over the business can sometimes be established more rapidly.

Insurgent criminal activity, of course, is not always confined to the territory under its control. In some instances, the insurgency has considerable international support. The LTTE, for example, has benefited enormously from the Tamil diaspora. Some of this took the form of donations that came simply from political sympathy for the cause; sometimes, however, "donations" were obtained through extortion. According to some reports in the mid-1990s, the LTTE had cells in as many as 38 countries in Europe, the Middle East, and North America.[66] These cells obtained financial support from the Tamil communities through voluntary contributions or intimidation and extortion. Reports in various countries including Canada reveal that LTTE supporters have engaged in extensive credit card fraud, social security fraud, counterfeiting, and extortion. In the late 1990s, the LTTE also diversified into alien smuggling and human trafficking. According to the Sri Lankan government, the Tamil Tigers used two shipping companies in an alien smuggling business that in 1999 alone moved 17,000 people to 11 countries.[67] Reportedly, this business earned $340 million. The government's assessment concluded that the operation was "one of the LTTE's major fund raising devices for its ongoing war with Sri Lankan government troops."[68]

The defeat of the LTTE, of course, revealed that even with multiple revenue streams, an insurgency can lose. Nevertheless, crime has become an essential source of funding and generally makes insurgencies more sustainable and more difficult for governments to defeat. When insurgents become involved in criminal activities, they are also more likely to become involved in some kind of cooperative relationship with criminal organizations concerned only about profit. As Thomas Naylor has acknowledged, "Any insurgency using the international black market to finance its activities inevitably forms mutually profitable and likely quite durable relations with international criminal groups."[69] The nature and scope of these relationships can now be examined.

RELATIONSHIPS BETWEEN INSURGENTS AND CRIMINAL ENTERPRISES

Assessing insurgency-criminal cooperation is similar in many respects to analyzing cooperation between criminal organizations and terrorist groups — or what is sometimes rather glibly termed the "organized crime-terrorism nexus." There are several different views on this. One important strand of thinking is that criminal organizations and terrorist groups are very different kinds of entities, driven by different objectives and different attitudes towards government, and operating in ways which make them anything but natural allies. As a leading Dutch criminologist and his co-author noted:

to real career criminals, the conduct of politically motivated terrorists appears incomprehensible if not down-
right "weird." Why would anyone take such extreme
risks without any prospect of getting rich in the end?
Who would want to openly confront the authorities
instead of evading or corrupting them? Is it not much
more sensible to keep illegal activities as low-key and
hidden as possible? Is it not foolish to draw attention
to yourself by using disproportional violence? The opportunities for organized crime are largely based on
the idea of exploiting the existing imperfections in the
economic and moral system of the state. . . . Viewed
from this perspective, organized crime is conservative.
Solving social and political problems would put it out
of business.[70]

On the other side, Tamara Makarenko complained
that the linkages are underestimated, noting that there
is a:

common reticence within the academic community to
consider arguments which go contrary to the widely
accepted view that criminal and terrorist groups have
no interest in cooperating because any interaction is
faced with inherent risks associated with trust, loyalty, divergent views on the necessity of the state, and
transaction costs which naturally increases vulnerabil-
ity of both sides to the authorities.[71]

The issue is not so much whether or not there are
cooperative linkages— obviously there are some—but
under what conditions and to what extent criminals
and insurgents are likely to cooperate with one another.

In terms of conditions, one possibility is cooperation in the early stages of insurgency. Criminals and
insurgents often come out of the same social milieu,
know each other, and might even trust one another.

In some cases in Southeast Asia and India, insurgent groups have even used existing organized crime structures as "building blocks exploiting both existing 'bandit' groups and smuggling routes and infrastructures as support systems for their movements."[72] Family or clan relationships facilitate this kind of co-option.[73]

Closely linked to this, cooperation also takes place when insurgent organizations and criminal enterprises have a natural affinity for one another. In Chechnya, for example, criminal enterprises and Chechen rebels during the 1990s shared a hatred of Russia. With both grounded in what Shultz and Dew termed "the unifying forces of tribalism and nationalism,"[74] cooperation was both easy and natural whenever insurgent interests and criminal interests coincided. The relationship between the Kosovo Liberation Army (KLA) and Albanian criminals was equally close. In fact, it was not simply a matter of commonality of interests between the KLA and Albanian criminal organizations. Rather, it was a matter of blurred identities and overlapping and perhaps even common membership. As Xavier Raufer has argued, there was:

> no way to distinguish Albanian guerrillas from local mafia groups. They have the same mindset and share the same goals. There's not such a thing as rebels and militias on the one hand and the Albanian mafia on the other. In the Albanian world . . . you have clans . . . and in those clans you have a mix of young men fighting for the cause of national liberation, young men belonging to the mafia, young men driving their cousins or other girls from the village into prostitution. It's absolutely impossible to distinguish between them. They obey the same clans, they have the same logic, the same world view, and to discriminate between one guy who is one day selling heroin and the next day fighting in the mountains is absolutely impossible.[75]

Insurgent groups and criminal organizations also tend to cooperate, sometimes explicitly and sometimes tacitly, where they are co-located and share an interest in limiting the power and reach of government forces. Co-location can be understood in two overlapping ways—geographical (i.e., territorial) space and opportunity space. Iraq provided some very interesting examples of such cooperation, especially in the kidnapping business, with "many credible reports suggesting that hostages, in particular foreign nationals, taken by criminal gangs" were subsequently "handed over to armed political groups in exchange for money."[76] With kidnapping gangs and insurgent and jihadi groups operating in the same space, some kind of relationship was inevitable. The relationship could have been one of rivalry and competition, but seems instead to have been one of tacit and explicit cooperation. Sometimes the initiative was taken by the kidnapping gangs, which would abduct people in the expectation that they could sell them to the political groups that might either kill or ransom them. So long as the kidnapping gangs were paid, the fate of the hostages was irrelevant.

On other occasions, however, the insurgency and jihadi groups let it be known that they had certain requirements or targets; the for-profit kidnapping group typically responded to what was, in effect, a request for services by abducting the appropriate kind of victim. "As the kidnap industry . . . matured, investigators saw cooperation evolve among criminal groups, and between them and the insurgency. Victims are sometimes sold and resold, gaining value each time."[77] In other words, the criminal market worked very efficiently and successfully, fully corroborating John Robb's conclusion that it operated as a bazaar of violence.[78] Something very similar seems to have occurred in Afghanistan where, as Matthieu Aikins has noted, the burgeoning kidnapping industry has become a key part of the conflict economy.[79] As in Iraq, foreigners are the most lucrative target for kidnapping, but not the most frequent targets.

In some respects, kidnapping in Iraq and Afghanistan is simply one example of the kind of cooperation that can occur when insurgencies become heavily engaged in criminal markets as either suppliers or customers of the criminal organizations. Indeed, it is when insurgencies engage in do-it-yourself organized crime that they are most likely to cooperate with criminal organizations. As noted above, when FARC became involved in processing cocaine, it was only a small step to supplying the drugs to trafficking organizations. Similarly in Afghanistan, as the Taliban has become more involved in the opium and heroin trade, it has established closer ties with drug trafficking organizations ranging from those operating out of Quetta in Pakistan to Russian and Tajik criminal organizations which traffic the heroin into the states of the former Soviet Union.

How these relationships are to be accurately characterized is a critical issue. They probably range from market suppliers and customers, to tactical alliances and perhaps even to strategic alliances. Market transactions, of course, can take the form not only of goods but also of services. As insurgents become more involved in criminal activities, their need for facilitated travel and transportation increases, and they will sometimes turn to what have been termed "criminal service providers" for the provision of items such as false documentation and forged passports.[80]

In some cases, cooperation is little more than an ad hoc response to convergent need on the one side and opportunity on the other, not progressing beyond a single transaction. In other cases, though, transactions might be regularized and routine, resulting in the development of trust and even the emergence of a tactical alliance to carry out certain kinds of mutually beneficial activities. In a few cases, the cooperation will become so extensive and the relationship so profitable and enduring that it is legitimate to refer to it as a strategic alliance. Although Naylor is skeptical of claims that there are strategic alliances between insurgents and criminal organizations, in some cases criminal enterprises and insurgencies not only engage in systematic and extensive cooperation but also expect to continue doing so in the future. Such strategic alliances transcend the vagaries of the market and generally involve either high levels of trust or sufficiently profitable cooperative ventures that both parties are fully committed to their continuation and even their deepening.

Most of these relationships have a degree of mutuality with benefits accruing to both parties. In some instances, however, there might be one-sided exploitation without any explicit or even tacit cooperation and perhaps no awareness by one of the parties that it is going on. Exploitation by criminals of insurgent-held territory for trafficking, for example, offers a natural protection from interdiction by government forces. In Sri Lanka, traffickers of illicit commodities such as drugs brought these commodities into the country through LTTE-held territory.[81] It is not clear that the LTTE was always aware of this and able to impose regular taxes on the goods and their transportation. It might well have been inadvertent and even unwitting facilitation by the LTTE. If insurgent groups are aware of such activities and impose a tax on those operating in the geographical areas under their control but offer nothing in return, then the relationship is simply one of predator and victim. A step up from this is a symbiotic or mutually beneficial relationship in which the payment of protection taxes is reciprocated by real protection against the forces of the state or even more overt facilitation of some kind.

One way of seeing these cooperative relationships is in terms of enhancing social capital. In this connection, Ronald Burt has identified a tradeoff that faces all organizations, both licit and illicit, between what he terms closure and brokerage.[82] On the one hand, organizations need closure for cohesion and trust; on the other they need brokerage for openness, vision, and access to additional resources. Both insurgent and criminal organizations have to be concerned about security and consequently form relatively closed groups, which seek to instill loyalty. By reaching out to one another, however, they can both obtain assets which would otherwise be unavailable.

Yet, there are also likely to be different positions and preferences regarding both the wisdom and the benefits of cooperating with different kinds of organizations. As suggested above, pragmatic criminals and political or ideological militants are not natural bedfellows, and working together is unlikely to be endorsed by all. Unfortunately, little is known about the internal deliberations of either insurgent groups or criminal enterprises regarding cooperation. Nevertheless, it is possible to identify a range of positions on cooperation: some within insurgencies will want to avoid it; others will adopt a more pragmatic approach, advocating cooperation when the benefits outweigh risks and it can be done without attracting much attention; while yet others will see it as a natural synergy—especially if the groups, in spite of divergent objectives, came out of the same environment. Those who object are likely to do so because of concerns that the link with criminals might taint the movement and reduce its political appeal. These concerns are not without merit.

The Slippery Slope of Criminality.

Insurgents engaged in criminal activities or co-operation with criminals to fund their programs of political violence and their ideological objectives face several dangers, including the loss of cohesion. Money can be a divisive as well as unifying force within an insurgency. Indeed, divisions can arise over the distribution of money as well as its source. While distribution issues can become highly contentious, arguments over the source of funds are often more fundamental as they center on the very nature of the insurgency; an even more serious problem than the loss of cohesion is the loss of political identity. Generally, insurgents are fighting for a cause that is related to the removal of the existing government and its replacement with a form of government based on different norms, values, and principles. In most cases, insurgents seek to establish the dominance of distinctive ideas of social justice and the redistribution of resources within society in accordance with those principles. With left-wing insurgents, the struggle is to replace what is seen as elite dominance and exploitation with social egalitarianism. In the case of insurgency inspired by religion, the aim is usually to replace secular government with a government based on religious fundamentalism or one kind of sectarian dominance with another kind.

These objectives are not easily reconciled with the widespread use of criminal activities, and even though criminal activities are typically justified in some ways (for example, Islamic insurgents typically condemn drug consumption but accept drug trafficking on the grounds that the infidel is both customer and target), such justifications can all too easily smack of hypocrisy. Moreover, as Naylor has argued, "The lure of quick wealth can on occasion cause a guerilla organization . . . to degenerate into simple criminality."[83] The acquisition of funds as a means to an end can become an end in itself. The result is distraction from the cause.

In extreme cases, this leads to a transformation from insurgent group to criminal enterprise, the cause be damned. The Pentagon Gang in the Philippines is a case in point. Made up of former Moro National Liberation Front (MNLF) and Moro Islamic Liberation Front (MILF) rebels, The Pentagon Gang has become predominantly a criminal organization that has made considerable money through kidnapping for ransom. Although some observers claim that the Pentagon Gang is the fund-raising arm of the MILF, the MILF has denied this and in July 2009 actually apprehended a Pentagon Gang member responsible for kidnapping a 4-year-old Chinese boy.[84] Another example is FARC. One indication of the transformation was the opulence of some of FARC's jungle locations, which suggested that the organization had become less ideological and more mercenary. Indeed, some observers now believe that FARC has both transformed and fragmented from a cohesive insurgency united by ideological beliefs and aspirations, to a set of drug trafficking organizations animated by nothing other than the desire for profit. In effect, those who were concerned that FARC's involvement in the drug business would compromise its ideological purity were proved correct. This was not unprecedented. Some years earlier, the Burmese Communist Party had also succumbed to what Naylor described as "the corrupting influence of narcotics money."[85]

Closely related to the loss of the insurgency's identity (which is essentially internal) is the loss of its legitimacy in the wider community. Insurgents fight for what they typically see as loftily unselfish goals: they are using violence on behalf of principles or ideological mandates. From this perspective, the use of criminal activity for funding is a two-edged sword. It can enhance the sustainability of the organization but can also diminish the level of its support. A good example of this occurred in Iraq where Jaish-al-Mahdi (a militia which was at times involved in the insurgency but also became the protector of large segments of the Shia population in Baghdad) became so predatory in its criminal activities that many of its erstwhile supporters and constituents became disillusioned. In response, JAM sought to reestablish its legitimacy with a large part of the Shia population by purging the most egregious criminals from its ranks.

Criminal behavior has also become a problem for the Taliban in Afghanistan, with one analyis claiming that banditry, extortion, bribery, and all-out criminality "have undermined Taliban tactics and strategy" and corrupted "the organization from the district level on up, likely infecting provincial level leadership as well."[86] Fortunately for the Taliban, however, government corruption is widely seen as even more pervasive, disruptive, and exploitative. Consequently, the Taliban has not had the same kind of legitimacy crisis that confronted JAM in Iraq.

In some cases, the reliance on criminal activities offers opportunities for governments either to drive wedges or make deals, with the result that the insurgents give up their campaigns of violence in return for being able continue with their criminal enterprises. Ironically, the more important criminal activities become, the greater the prospects for deal-making—as highlighted by Richard Snyder in his analysis of lootable resources.[87] Snyder notes that although lootable resources sometimes contribute to disorder, they can also contribute to order. As he notes, in Burma during the 1990s "a major expansion of the narcotics industry" was accompanied not by growing violence, but by "the ending of civil war, demobilization of insurgents, and the successful restoration of a military regime's grip on power."[88] In his view, "the opium boom contributed to the emergence of political order in the 1990s because (a) opium provided a lucrative 'exit option' for rebels, making it easier for the military to demobilize them; and (b) the military built institutions of joint extraction with the erstwhile rebels that gave it a large share of opium revenues."[89] A tacit social contract in which insurgent groups were allowed to continue their drug trafficking activities in return for the cessation of violence was subsequently extended to allow drug proceeds to be invested in the economy. Consequently, former insurgent drug lords such as Lo Hsing Han and Khun Sa became major entrepreneurs investing in hotels, casinos, and various other businesses.[90]

The other danger for an insurgency is that if tensions arise about the distribution of the spoils of criminal activity among various factions, this provides opportunities for wedge-driving. This is particularly the case in a composite insurgency. Control over smuggling activities, for example, became a major point of contention in the Iraq insurgency as al-Qaeda in Iraq (AQI) sought to take over control of the traditional smuggling and black market activities of the Sunni tribes and to appropriate most of the proceeds from these activities. These tensions between AQI and the tribes created major opportunities for the United States. The result was the Anbar Awakening and the defeat of AQI in the province.[91] Another facet of this dispute was that the insurgency had become a source of employment. By creating and paying for the Sons of Iraq, which for most intents and purposes was a Sunni militia, the United States, in effect, outbid AQI. Even so, AQI continued to use criminal activities such as car theft, kidnapping, and extortion to maintain its resistance in and around Mosul and several other places.

The implication of the preceding analysis is that insurgents' resort to criminal activities for funding and the development of linkages with criminal enterprises can be a double-edged sword, both perpetuating and weakening insurgency at the same time. The tensions created by criminal activity are sometimes even reflected in the aftermath of insurgency. Naylor notes, for example, that "after the end of the Huk rebellion in the Philippines in 1950 . . . some elements took to the hills to engage in social banditry, redistributing stolen wealth among poor peasants, while others settled down near U.S. military bases to collect rake-offs from the gambling and prostitution rackets. . . ."[92] In effect, some of the insurgents remained true to their ideals while others found that the fund-raising skills they had developed during the insurgency could be put to good use for personal enrichment after the conflict.

FINAL REFLECTIONS

Throughout this chapter, an attempt has been made to offer analytic clarity through a set of carefully drawn terminology and conceptual distinctions as related to insurgencies and organized crime. A difficulty is, of course, that the analysis tends to categorize and conceptualize the actors and the issues in a manner that may strike as overly neat and indifferent to difficult loose ends. For example, in this KLA scenario, insurgents and criminals, in part at least, are labels imposed from outside and are not necessarily synonymous with the ways in which members of insurgencies or criminal organizations see themselves.[93] The emphasis here has been on distinctions and conceptual constructs. Yet terrorists, insurgents, and criminals are not bound by these distinctions and differentiations. Instead, they have their own reality, their own imperatives, and their own logic, all of which are internally driven rather than externally imposed. There is clearly an important distinction between activities which are oriented towards profits and those which are political—and in some cases engaging in the former will erode and compromise the latter. Yet, there are also actors who manage to engage in both activities and see no tension between them. Being a greedy criminal is not necessarily incompatible with being a committed terrorist or insurgent.

If this idea is accepted, then it is necessary to consider not only the relationships outlined above—relationships between different kinds of entities and between entities and activities—but also the possibility that new kinds of hybrid organizations have emerged, are emerging, or will emerge in the future. Some of these hybrid organizations have a dual agenda, simultaneously pursuing both political and financial objectives and seemingly managing both pursuits successfully. In effect, both motives and methods are mixed in ways that do not fit the traditional and existing categories. Some commentators are groping towards analysis of these hybrids. Justine Rosenthal, for example, has used the term "for-profit terrorism," which initially seems an oxymoron but actually captures what could well be an emerging reality.[94] Indeed, Daewood Ibrahim, leader of D-company, seems to be both a very successful criminal entrepreneur and, on some occasions at least, a terrorist and/or terrorist facilitator.[95] Similarly, the notion of warlords seems to involve dual objectives. In both Africa and Southeast Asia, some groups seem to have transformed over time from ideological insurgency to warlords whose underlings are there for a job, not a cause. As Lawrence Cline put it, their violence and brutality do not accord with what he terms the "cleaner models" of criminal organizations.[96] Yet such groups need to be accounted for. Groups like the Lord's Resistance Army in Uganda seem to have little reason for continued existence aside from looting and the opportunity to make survival money, and seem to be located somewhere between insurgents, criminal organizations, and anomic violence.[97] Whatever the case, they seem unlikely to disappear anytime soon. Similarly, some hybrids — and Abu Sayyaf might fit here — seem to be in an interim stage of metamorphosis. Yet it is not inevitable that what appears to be a transformation from one type of organization to another will actually be completed. The problem for analysts is that what currently appears to be an interim stage between groups with clear identities and objectives might well prove to be as enduring as it is uncomfortable.

ENDNOTES - CHAPTER 2

1. The author has benefitted enormously from discussions with Dr. Steven Metz and Dr. Lawrence Cline about many of the issues discussed in this chapter. Dr. Michael Echemendia, Dr. Lindsay Clutterbuck, and Robert Perito also provided very useful comments on an earlier draft of this chapter. All sins of omission and commission remain those of the author alone.

2. Charles Tilly, "War Making and the State as Organized Crime," in Peter B. Evans, Dietrich Rueschemeyer, and Theda Skocpol, eds., *Bringing the State Back In*, Cambridge, UK: Cambridge University Press, 1985, pp. 170-171.

3. Steven Metz, *The Future of Insurgency*, Carlisle, PA: Strategic Studies Institute, U.S. Army War College, December 10, 1993, available from *www.au.af.mil/au/awc/awcgate/ssi/metz.pdf*.

4. Gretchen Peters, *The Seeds of Terror*, New York: St Martin's, 2009. See also Svante Cornell, "Narcotics and Armed Conflict: Interaction and Implications," *Studies in Conflict and Terrorism*, Vol. 30, 2007, pp. 207-227.

5. Vanda Felbab-Brown, *Shooting Up*, Washington, DC: Brookings Institution Press, November 2009.

6. William Noel Ivey, "Robin Hood or Al Capone: Natural Resources and Conflict in India's Naxalite Insurgency," in Magnus Oberg and Kaare Strom, eds., *Resources, Governance and Civil Conflict*, London, UK: Routledge, 2007.

7. On the issue of greed and grievance, see Mats Berdal and David Malone, eds., *Greed and Grievance: Economic Agendas in Civil Wars*, Boulder, CO: Lynne Rienner, 2000. See also Richard Snyder, "Does Lootable Wealth Breed Disorder? A Political Economy of Extraction Framework," *Comparative Political Studies*, Vol. 39, No. 8, October 2006, pp. 943-968.

8. Snyder, p. 943.

9. Lyubov Mincheva and Ted Robert Gurr, "How Trans-state Terrorism and International Crime Make Common Cause," Paper

presented at the Annual Meeting of the International Studies Association, Panel on Comparative Perspectives on States, Terrorism and Crime, San Diego, March 24, 2006; Chris Dishman, "Terrorism, Crime, and Transformation," *Studies in Conflict and Terrorism*, Vol. 24, No.1, 2001, pp. 43-58; Chester G. Oehme III, "Terrorists, Insurgents, and Criminals—Growing Nexus?" *Studies in Conflict & Terrorism*, Vol. 31, No. 1, pp. 80-93.

10. R. Thomas Naylor, *Wages of Crime: Black Markets, Illegal Finance, and the Underworld Economy*, Ithaca, NY: Cornell University Press, 2002, pp. 44-87.

11. Felbab-Brown, *Shooting Up*.

12. David Kilcullen, *The Accidental Guerilla*, New York: Oxford, 2009.

13. Jeremy Weinstein, *Inside Rebellion: The Politics of Insurgent Violence*, Cambridge, MA: Harvard University Press: 2006.

14. See Tamara Makarenko, "Transnational Crime and Its Evolving Links to Terrorism and Instability," *Jane's Intelligence Review*, Vol. 13, No. 11, November 2001; and Tamara Makarenko, "Transnational Crime and Terrorism: the Emerging Nexus," in Paul Smith, ed., *Transnational Violence and Seams of Lawlessness in the Asia-Pacific*, New York: M. E. Sharpe, 2004.

15. Thomas X. Hammes, "Countering Evolved Insurgent Networks," *Military Review*, July-August 2006, pp. 18-26.

16. Phil Williams, "Terrorist Financing and Organized Crime: Nexus, Appropriation or Transformation?" in Thomas Biersteker and Susan Eckert, eds., *Countering the Financing of Terrorism*, London, UK: Routledge, 2008, pp. 126-149.

17. Behsat Ekici, Phil Williams, and Ayhan Akbulut, "The PKK and the KDNs: Cooperation, Convergence or Conflict?" forthcoming.

18. This is based on conversations with Peruvian officials, July 2009.

19. Pablo G. Dreyfus, "Peru and Sendero Luminoso (1980-1990): Narcoterrorism Personified?" Paper presented at the annual Midwest meeting of the International Studies Association, Cleveland, Ohio, October 3-5, 1997, p. 36.

20. Doris Aguirre, "Shining Path Leader 'Dalton' Admits Alliance of Terrorists with Drug Traffickers," *La Republica Online,* April 24, 2009.

21. John Sullivan, "State of Siege: Mexico's Criminal Insurgency," *Small Wars Journal*, available from *www.smallwarsjournal. com.*

22. Karl Weick and Kathleen Sutcliffe, *Managing the Unexpected: Assuring High Performance in an Age of Uncertainty,* San Francisco, CA: Jossey-Bass, 2001.

23. See John T. Picarelli, "The Turbulent Nexus of Transnational Organized Crime And Terrorism: A Theory of Malevolent International Relations," *Global Crime*, Vol. 7, No. 1, February 2006, pp. 1-24.

24. Naylor, p. 53.

25. Alexus G. Grynkewich, "Welfare as Warfare: How Violent Non-State Groups Use Social Services to Attack the State," *Studies in Conflict & Terrorism*, Vol. 31, No. 4, 2008, pp. 350–370.

26. See Michael Kenney, *From Pablo to Osama*, University Park, PA: Pennsylvania State University Press, 2007.

27. Naylor, p. 56.

28. *Ibid.*, pp. 55-56.

29. *Ibid.*, p. 56.

30. Mincheva and Gurr.

31. Ingrid A. Parker, *Understanding the Links Between Organized Crime and Terrorism in Military Operations*, Fort Leavenworth, KS: U.S. Army Command and General Staff College, 2007, pp. 61-62.

32. Hammes.

33. Naylor, pp. 60-62.

34. *Ibid.*

35. This is discussed more fully in Phil Williams, *Criminals, Militias and Insurgents: Organized Crime in Iraq*, Carlisle, PA: Strategic Studies Institute, U.S. Army War College, August 2009, p. 132.

36. "Iraqi Newspaper Says Kidnapping Becomes Profitable Trade," *Al Shira*, Baghdad, in Arabic, October 2, 2004.

37. Daniel McGrory, "How $45m Secretly Bought Freedom of Foreign Hostages," *The Times*, London, UK, May 22, 2006, p. 8.

38. This figure is based on an average payment of $10,000 per hostage, which is more likely to be a low rather than high estimate.

39. Naylor, p. 66.

40. "Guerilla Miners: The FARC Turns to Gold," *The Economist*, January 27, 2011.

41. Naylor, p. 66.

42. Diego Gambetta, *The Sicilian Mafia: The Business of Private Protection*, Cambridge, MA: Harvard University Press, 1993.

43. Gretchen Peters, *Crime and Insurgency in the Tribal Areas of Afghanistan and Pakistan*, West Point, NY: The Combating Terrorism Center at West Point, Harmony Project, October 15, 2010, p. 12.

44. Naylor, p. 70.

45. See Metz. The author is also grateful to a capstone seminar on organized crime and terrorism held at the University of Pittsburgh, Pittsburgh, PA, in which Erin Wick's research on FARC was particularly helpful.

46. *The World Geopolitics of Drugs 1998/99,* Paris, France: Observatoire Geopolitique Des Drogues, April 2000.

47. *Ibid.,* p. 143.

48. Drug Enforcement Administration (DEA), "United States Charges 50 Leaders of Narco-Terrorist FARC in Colombia With Supplying More Than Half of The World's Cocaine," News Release, March 22, 2006, available from *www.justice.gov/dea/pubs/ pressrel/pr032206a.html.*

49. DEA, "Two FARC Associates Plead to Drug Conspiracy Charges," New Release, September 28, 2006, available from *www. justice.gov/dea/pubs/states/newsrel/mia092806.html* .

50. *Ibid.*

51. James Cockayne and Phil Williams, *The Invisible Tide: Towards an International Strategy to Deal with Drug Trafficking through West Africa,* New York: International Peace Institute, forthcoming .

52. See Tamara Makarenko, "Crime, Terror, and the Central Asian Drug Trade," *Harvard Asia Quarterly,* Vol. 6, No. 3, 2002, available from *asiaquarterly.com/2006/01/28/ii-88/.*

53. Svante Cornell, "Narcotics, Radicalism and Armed Conflict in Central Asia: The Islamic Movement of Uzbekistan," *Terrorism and Political Violence,* Vol. 17, 2005, pp. 619-639, especially p. 632.

54. This seizure was even used as a recruiting and training tool by the Uzbek customs.

55. Peters, *Seeds of Terror,* p. 110.

56. Taylor, p. 57.

57. Peters, *Seeds of Terror,* pp. 116, 123.

58. *Ibid.*

59. See G. H. Peires, "Clandestine Transactions of the LTTE and the Secessionist Campaign in Sri Lanka," available from *www.ices.lk/publications/esr/articles_jan01/2001(1)-Peiris.rtf.*

60. Naylor, p. 73.

61. Louise Shelley, "The Unholy Trinity: Transnational Crime, Corruption and Terrorism," *Brown Journal of World Affairs*, Vol. 11, No. 2, Winter-Spring 2005, pp. 101-111.

62. Pratap Chatterjee, "Mystery of the Missing Meters: Accounting for Iraq's Oil Revenue," March 22, 2007, available from *www.corpwatch.org/article.php?id=14427.*

63. For a fuller discussion, see Williams, *Criminals, Militias and Insurgents.*

64. *Ibid.*

65. *Ibid.*

66. *Funding Terror: The Liberation Tigers of Tamil Eelam and their Criminal Activities in Canada and the Western World,* Toronto, Canada: Mackenzie Institute, 1996.

67. "Sri Lanka: Sri Lanka's Rebels Involved In Trafficking Human Cargo," *Xinhua News Agency*, April 7, 2000.

68. *Ibid.*

69. Naylor, p. 23.

70. Frank Bovenkerk and Bashir Abou Chakra, "Terrorism and Organized Crime," *Forum on Crime and Society*, Vol. 4, Nos. 1 and 2, December 2004, pp. 3-16, especially p. 12.

71. Tamara Makarenko, "Criminal and Terrorist Networks: Gauging Interaction and the Resultant Impact on Terrorism," Center for Transatlantic Relations, available from *www.docstoc.com/docs/79694373/Criminal-and-Terrorist-Networks-Gauging--Interaction-and-the.*

72. I am grateful for this observation made to me in a personal communication by Lawrence Cline.

73. *Ibid.*

74. Richard H. Shultz and Andrea S. Dew, *Insurgents, Terrorists and Militias*, New York: Columbia University Press, 2006, p. 137.

75. Xavier Raufer, quoted in Jamie Dettmer, "Heroin and Sex Trade Fuel Albanian Nationalism," *Insight on the News*, August 13, 2001.

76. AI report, July 25, 2005, quoted in Home Office, UK, "Country of Origin Information Report: Iraq," October 31, 2006.

77. Kirk Semple, "Kidnapped in Iraq: Victim's Tale of Clockwork Death and Ransom," *New York Times*, May 7, 2006, p. 11.

78. John Robb, *Brave New War*, New York, Wiley, 2007.

79. Matthieu Aikins, "The Big Business of Kidnapping in Afghanistan," AfPak Channel, Foreign Policy, available from *afpak. foreignpolicy.com/posts/2010/10/20/the_big_business_of_kidnapping_ in_afghanistan*.

80. I am grateful to Deborah Diamond for this term.

81. Interview with Sri Lankan official, Kathmandu, Nepal, in August 2008.

82. Ronald Burt, *Brokerage and Closure: An Introduction to Social Capital*, New York: Oxford University Press, 2000.

83. Naylor, p. 57.

84. "MILF admits holding alleged kidnap gang chief," *Inquirer*, Mindanao, July 4, 2009.

85. Naylor, p. 71.

86. *Understanding Afghan Culture: Analyzing the Taliban Code of Conduct: Reinventing the Layeha*, National Security Report, Monterey, CA: Naval Postgraduate School, 2009, p. 10, available from *info.publicintelligence.net/Layeha.pdf*.

87. Richard Snyder, "Does Lootable Wealth Breed Disorder?" *Comparative Political Studies*, Vol. 39, No. 8, October 2006, pp. 943-968.

88. *Ibid.*, p. 944.

89. *Ibid.*, p. 959.

90. The U.S. Government was very critical of this, alleging that the Burmese government was encouraging or condoning money laundering. See Bureau for International Narcotics and Law Enforcement Affairs, U.S. Department of State, *International Narcotics Control Strategy Report, 1999*, Washington, DC, March 2000.

91. Austin Long, "The Anbar Awakening," *Survival*, Vol. 50, No. 2, April 2008, pp. 67-94, especially p. 77.

92. Naylor, p. 57.

93. I am grateful to Louise Shelley, who made this observation in relationship to nuclear material trafficking in Georgia at a conference on proliferation networks held at the Naval Postgraduate School in Monterey, CA. The author would like to thank James Cockayne for emphasizing the importance of labeling.

94. Justine A. Rosenthal, "For-Profit Terrorism: The Rise of Armed Entrepreneurs," *Studies in Conflict and Terrorism*, Vol. 31, No. 6, 2008, pp. 481-498.

95. See "Profile: India's fugitive gangster," *BBC News*, September 12, 2006, available from *news.bbc.co.uk/2/hi/south_asia/4775531.stm*.

96. Cline, personal communication.

97. *Ibid.* See also Lawrence E. Cline, "Spirits and the Cross: Religiously Based Violence Movements in Uganda," *Small Wars and Insurgencies*, Vol. 14, No. 2, Summer 2003, pp. 113-130.

www.ingramcontent.com/pod-product-compliance
Lightning Source LLC
Chambersburg PA
CBHW072339290526
45794CB00002B/933